Algernon Charles Swinburne

Songs of Two Nations

Algernon Charles Swinburne

Songs of Two Nations

ISBN/EAN: 9783744775656

Printed in Europe, USA, Canada, Australia, Japan

Cover: Foto ©Thomas Meinert / pixelio.de

More available books at **www.hansebooks.com**

BY

ALGERNON CHARLES SWINBURNE

London

CHATTO AND WINDUS, PICCADILLY

1875

LONDON : PRINTED BY
SPOTTISWOODE AND CO., NEW-STREET SQUARE
AND PARLIAMENT STREET

I saw the double-featured statue stand
Of Memnon or of Janus, half with night
Veiled, and fast bound with iron; half with light
Crowned, holding all men's future in his hand.

And all the old westward face of time grown grey
Was writ with cursing and inscribed for death
But on the face that met the morning's breath
Fear died of hope as darkness dies of day.

CONTENTS.

A SONG OF ITALY.

B

INSCRIBED

WITH ALL DEVOTION AND REVERENCE

TO

JOSEPH MAZZINI.

1867.

A SONG OF ITALY.

UPON a windy night of stars that fell
    At the wind's spoken spell,
Swept with sharp strokes of agonizing light
    From the clear gulf of night,
Between the fixed and fallen glories one
    Against my vision shone,
More fair and fearful and divine than they
    That measure night and day,
And worthier worship ; and within mine eyes
    The formless folded skies
Took shape and were unfolded like as flowers.
    And I beheld the hours
As maidens, and the days as labouring men,
    And the soft nights again
As wearied women to their own souls wed,
    And ages as the dead.
And over these living, and them that died,
    From one to the other side
A lordlier light than comes of earth or air
    Made the world's future fair.
A woman like to love in face, but not
    A thing of transient lot—

And like to hope, but having hold on truth—
    And like to joy or youth,
Save that upon the rock her feet were set—
    And like what men forget,
Faith, innocence, high thought, laborious peace—
    And yet like none of these,
Being not as these are mortal, but with eyes
    That sounded the deep skies
And clove like wings or arrows their clear way
    Through night and dawn and day—
So fair a presence over star and sun
    Stood, making these as one.
For in the shadow of her shape were all
    Darkened and held in thrall,
So mightier rose she past them ; and I felt
    Whose form, whose likeness knelt
With covered hair and face and clasped her knees ;
    And knew the first of these
Was Freedom, and the second Italy.
    And what sad words said she
For mine own grief I knew not, nor had heart
    Therewith to bear my part
And set my songs to sorrow ; nor to hear
    How tear by sacred tear
Fell from her eyes as flowers or notes that fall
    In some slain feaster's hall
Where in mid music and melodious breath
    Men singing have seen death.
So fair, so lost, so sweet she knelt ; or so
    In our lost eyes below

Seemed to us sorrowing ; and her speech being said,
  Fell, as one who falls dead.
And for a little she too wept, who stood
  Above the dust and blood
And thrones and troubles of the world ; then spake,
  As who bids dead men wake.

' Because the years were heavy on thy head ;
  Because dead things are dead ;
Because thy chosen on hill-side, city and plain
  Are shed as drops of rain ;
Because all earth was black, all heaven was blind,
  And we cast out of mind ;
Because men wept, saying *Freedom*, knowing of thee,
  Child, that thou wast not free :
Because wherever blood was not shame was
  Where thy pure foot did pass ;
Because on Promethean rocks distent
  Thee fouler eagles rent ;
Because a serpent stains with slime and foam
  This that is not thy Rome ;
Child of my womb, whose limbs were made in me,
  Have I forgotten thee?
In all thy dreams through all these years on wing,
  Hast thou dreamed such a thing?
The mortal mother-bird outsoars her nest,
  The child outgrows the breast ;
But suns as stars shall fall from heaven and cease,
  Ere we twain be as these ;

Yea, utmost skies forget their utmost sun,
  Ere we twain be not one.
My lesser jewels sewn on skirt and hem,
  I have no heed of them
Obscured and flawed by sloth or craft or power;
  But thou, that wast my flower,
The blossom bound between my brows and worn
  In sight of even and morn
From the last ember of the flameless west
  To the dawn's baring breast—
I were not Freedom if thou wert not free,
  Nor thou wert Italy.
O mystic rose ingrained with blood, impearled
  With tears of all the world !
The torpor of their blind brute-ridden trance
  Kills England and chills France ;
And Spain sobs hard through strangling blood; and
    snows
  Hide the huge eastern woes.
But thou, twin-born with morning, nursed of noon,
  And blessed of star and moon !
What shall avail to assail thee any more,
  From sacred shore to shore ?
Have Time and Love not knelt down at thy feet,
  Thy sore, thy soiled, thy sweet,
Fresh from the flints and mire of murderous ways
  And dust of travelling days ?
Hath Time not kissed them, Love not washed them
    fair,
  And wiped with tears and hair ?

Though God forget thee, I will not forget;
  Though heaven and earth be set
Against thee, O unconquerable child,
  Abused, abased, reviled,
Lift thou not less from no funereal bed
  Thine undishonoured head ;
Love thou not less, by lips of thine once prest,
  This my now barren breast ;
Seek thou not less, being well assured thereof,
  O child, my latest love.
For now the barren bosom shall bear fruit,
  Songs leap from lips long mute,
And with my milk the mouths of nations fed
  Again be glad and red
That were worn white with hunger and sorrow and
     thirst ;
And thou, most fair and first,
Thou whose warm hands and sweet live lips I feel
  Upon me for a seal,
Thou whose least looks, whose smiles and little sighs,
  Whose passionate pure eyes,
Whose dear fair limbs that neither bonds could
     bruise
  Nor hate of men misuse,
Whose flower-like breath and bosom, O my child,
  O mine and undefiled,
Fill with such tears as burn like bitter wine
  These mother's eyes of mine,
Thrill with huge passions and primeval pains
  The fulness of my veins.

O sweetest head seen higher than any stands,
   I touch thee with mine hands,
I lay my lips upon thee, O thou most sweet,
   To lift thee on thy feet
And with the fire of mine to fill thine eyes ;
   I say unto thee, Arise.'

She ceased, and heaven was full of flame and sound,
   And earth's old limbs unbound
Shone and waxed warm with fiery dew and seed
   Shed through her at this her need :
And highest in heaven, a mother and full of grace,
   With no more covered face,
With no more lifted hands and bended knees,
   Rose, as from sacred seas
Love, when old time was full of plenteous springs,
   That fairest-born of things,
The land that holds the rest in tender thrall
   For love's sake in them all,
That binds with words and holds with eyes and
      hands
   All hearts in all men's lands.
So died the dream whence rose the live desire
   That here takes form and fire,
A spirit from the splendid grave of sleep
   Risen, that ye should not weep,
Should not weep more nor ever, O ye that hear
   And ever have held her dear,
Seeing now indeed she weeps not who wept sore,
   And sleeps not any more.

Hearken ye towards her, O people, exalt your eyes;
    Is this a thing that dies?

Italia! by the passion of the pain
    That bent and rent thy chain;
Italia! by the breaking of the bands,
    The shaking of the lands;
Beloved, O men's mother, O men's queen,
    Arise, appear, be seen!
Arise, array thyself in manifold
    Queen's raiment of wrought gold;
With girdles of green freedom, and with red
    Roses, and white snow shed
Above the flush and frondage of the hills
    That all thy deep dawn fills
And all thy clear night veils and warms with wings
    Spread till the morning sings;
The rose of resurrection, and the bright
    Breast lavish of the light,
The lady lily like the snowy sky
    Ere the stars wholly die;
As red as blood, and whiter than a wave,
    Flowers grown as from thy grave,
From the green fruitful grass in Maytime hot,
    Thy grave, where thou art not.
Gather the grass and weave, in sacred sign
    Of the ancient earth divine,
The holy heart of things, the seed of birth,
    The mystical warm earth.
O thou her flower of flowers, with treble braid
    Be thy sweet head arrayed,

In witness of her mighty motherhood
  Who bore thee and found thee good,
Her fairest-born of children, on whose head
  Her green and white and red
Are hope and light and life, inviolate
  Of any latter fate.
Fly, O our flag, through deep Italian air,
  Above the flags that were,
The dusty shreds of shameful battle-flags
  Trampled and rent in rags,
As withering woods in autumn's bitterest breath
  Yellow, and black as death ;
Black as crushed worms that sicken in the sense,
  And yellow as pestilence.
Fly, green as summer and red as dawn and white
  As the live heart of light,
The blind bright womb of colour unborn, that brings
  Forth all fair forms of things,
As freedom all fair forms of nations dyed
  In divers-coloured pride.
Fly fleet as wind on every wind that blows
  Between her seas and snows,
From Alpine white, from Tuscan green, and where
  Vesuvius reddens air.
Fly ! and let all men see it, and all kings wail,
  And priests wax faint and pale,
And the cold hordes that moan in misty places
  And the funereal races
And the sick serfs of lands that wait and wane
  See thee and hate thee in vain.

In the clear laughter of all winds and waves,
   In the blown grass of graves,
In the long sound of fluctuant boughs of trees,
   In the broad breath of seas,
Bid the sound of thy flying folds be heard ;
   And as a spoken word
Full of that fair god and that merciless
   Who rends the Pythoness,
So be the sound and so the fire that saith
   She feels her ancient breath
And the old blood move in her immortal veins.

   Strange travail and strong pains,
Our mother, hast thou borne these many years
   While thy pure blood and tears
Mixed with the Tyrrhene and the Adrian sea ;
   Light things were said of thee,
As of one buried deep among the dead ;
   Yea, she hath been, they said,
She was when time was younger, and is not ;
   The very cerecloths rot
That flutter in the dusty wind of death,
   Not moving with her breath ;
Far seasons and forgotten years enfold
   Her dead corpse old and cold
With many windy winters and pale springs :
   She is none of this world's things.
Though her dead head like a live garland wear
   The golden-growing hair

That flows over her breast down to her feet,
   Dead queens, whose life was sweet
In sight of all men living, have been found
   So cold, so clad, so crowned,
With all things faded and with one thing fair,
   Their old immortal hair,
When flesh and bone turned dust at touch of day :
   And she is dead as they.

So men said sadly, mocking ; so the slave,
   Whose life was his soul's grave :
So, pale or red with change of fast and feast,
   The sanguine-sandalled priest
So the Austrian, when his fortune came to flood,
   And the warm wave was blood ;
With wings that widened and with beak that smote,
   So shrieked through either throat
From the hot horror of its northern nest
   That double-headed pest ;
So, triple-crowned with fear and fraud and shame,
   He of whom treason came,
The herdsman of the Gadarean swine ;
   So all his ravening kine,
Made fat with poisonous pasture ; so not we,
   Mother, beholding thee.
Make answer, O the crown of all our slain,
   Ye that were one, being twain,
Twain brethren, twin-born to the second birth,
   Chosen out of all our earth
To be the prophesying stars that say
   How hard is night on day,

Stars in serene and sudden heaven rerisen
 Before the sun break prison
And ere the moon be wasted ; fair first flowers
 In that red wreath of ours
Woven with the lives of all whose lives were shed
 To crown their mother's head
With leaves of civic cypress and thick yew,
 Till the olive bind it too,
Olive and laurel and all loftier leaves
 That victory wears or weaves
At her fair feet for her beloved brow ;
 Hear, for she too hears now,
O Pisacane, from Calabrian sands ;
 O all heroic hands
Close on the sword-hilt, hands of all her dead ;
 O many a holy head,
Bowed for her sake even to her reddening dust ;
 O chosen, O pure and just,
Who counted for a small thing life's estate,
 And died, and made it great ;
Ye whose names mix with all her memories ; ye
 Who rather chose to see
Death, than our more intolerable things ;
 Thou whose name withers kings,
Agesilao ; thou too, O chiefliest thou,
 The slayer of splendid brow,
Laid where the lying lips of fear deride
 The foiled tyrannicide,
Foiled, fallen, slain, scorned, and happy ; being in fame,
 Felice, like thy name,

Not like thy fortune ; father of the fight,
  Having in hand our light.
Ah, happy ! for that sudden-swerving hand
  Flung light on all thy land,
Yea, lit blind France with compulsory ray,
  Driven down a righteous way ;
Ah, happiest ! for from thee the wars began,
  From thee the fresh springs ran ;
From thee the lady land that queens the earth
  Gat as she gave new birth.
O sweet mute mouths, O all fair dead of ours,
  Fair in her eyes as flowers,
Fair without feature, vocal without voice,
  Strong without strength, rejoice !
Hear it with ears that hear not, and on eyes
  That see not let it rise,
Rise as a sundawn ; be it as dew that drips
  On dumb and dusty lips ;
Eyes have ye not, and see it ; neither ears,
  And there is none but hears.
This is the same for whom ye bled and wept ;
  She was not dead, but slept.
This is that very Italy which was
  And is and shall not pass.

But thou, though all were not well done, O chief,
  Must thou take shame or grief?
Because one man is not as thou or ten,
  Must thou take shame for men ?

Because the supreme sunrise is not yet,
  Is the young dew not wet?
Wilt thou not yet abide a little while,
  Soul without fear or guile,
Mazzini,—O our prophet, O our priest,
  A little while at least?
A little hour of doubt and of control,
  Sustain thy sacred soul ;
Withhold thine heart, our father, but an hour ;
  Is it not here, the flower,
Is it not blown and fragrant from the root,
  And shall not be the fruit?
Thy children, even thy people thou hast made,
  Thine, with thy words arrayed,
Clothed with thy thoughts and girt with thy desires,
  Yearn up toward thee as fires.
Art thou not father, O father, of all these?
  From thine own Genoese
To where of nights the lower extreme lagune
  Feels its Venetian moon,
Nor suckling's mouth nor mother's breast set free
  But hath that grace through thee.
The milk of life on death's unnatural brink
  Thou gavest them to drink,
The natural milk of freedom ; and again
  They drank, and they were men.
The wine and honey of freedom and of faith
  They drank, and cast off death.
Bear with them now ; thou art holier : yet endure,
  Till they as thou be pure.
                  c

Their swords at least that stemmed half Austria's tide
    Bade all its bulk divide ;
Else, though fate bade them for a breath's space fall,
    She had not fallen at all.
Not by their hands they made time's promise true ;
    Not by their hands, but through.
Nor on Custoza ran their blood to waste,
    Nor fell their fame defaced
Whom stormiest Adria with tumultuous tides
    Whirls undersea and hides.
Not his, who from the sudden-settling deck
    Looked over death and wreck
To where the mother's bosom shone, who smiled
    As he, so dying, her child ;
For he smiled surely, dying, to mix his death
    With her memorial breath ;
Smiled, being most sure of her, that in no wise,
    Die whoso will, she dies :
And she smiled surely, fair and far above,
    Wept not, but smiled for love.
Thou too, O splendour of the sudden sword
    That drove the crews abhorred
From Naples and the siren-footed strand,
    Flash from thy master's hand,
Shine from the middle summer of the seas
    To the old Æolides,
Outshine their fiery fumes of burning night,
    Sword, with thy midday light ;
Flame as a beacon from the Tyrrhene foam
    To the rent heart of Rome,

From the island of her lover and thy lord,
    Her saviour and her sword.
In the fierce year of failure and of fame,
    Art thou not yet the same
That wast as lightning swifter than all wings
    In the blind face of kings?
When priests took counsel to devise despair,
    And princes to forswear,
She clasped thee, O her sword and flag-bearer
    And staff and shield to her,
O Garibaldi; need was hers and grief,
    Of thee and of the chief,
And of another girt in arms to stand
    As good of hope and hand,
As high of soul and happy, albeit indeed
    The heart should burn and bleed,
So but the spirit shake not nor the breast
    Swerve, but abide its rest.
As theirs did and as thine, though ruin clomb
    The highest wall of Rome,
Though treason stained and spilt her lustral water,
    And slaves led slaves to slaughter,
And priests, praying and slaying, watched them pass
    From a strange France, alas,
That was not freedom ; yet when these were past
    Thy sword and thou stood fast,
Till new men seeing thee where Sicilian waves
    Hear now no sound of slaves,
And where thy sacred blood is fragrant still
    Upon the Bitter Hill,

c 2

Seeing by that blood one country saved and stained,
 Less loved thee crowned than chained,
And less now only than the chief: for he,
 Father of Italy,
Upbore in holy hands the babe new-born
 Through loss and sorrow and scorn,
Of no man led, of many men reviled ;
 Till lo, the new-born child
Gone from between his hands, and in its place,
 Lo, the fair mother's face.
Blessed is he of all men, being in one
 As father to her and son,
Blessed of all men living, that he found
 Her weak limbs bared and bound,
And in his arms and in his bosom bore,
 And as a garment wore
Her weight of want, and as a royal dress
 Put on her weariness.
As in faith's hoariest histories men read,
 The strong man bore at need
Through roaring rapids when all heaven was wild
 The likeness of a child
That still waxed greater and heavier as he trod,
 And altered, and was God.
Praise him, O winds that move the molten air,
 O light of days that were,
And light of days that shall be; land and sea,
 And heaven and Italy:
Praise him, O storm and summer, shore and wave,
 O skies and every grave ;

O weeping hopes, O memories beyond tears,
   O many and murmuring years,
O sounds far off in time and visions far,
   O sorrow with thy star,
And joy with all thy beacons; ye that mourn,
   And ye whose light is born;
O fallen faces, and O souls arisen,
   Praise him from tomb and prison,
Praise him from heaven and sunlight; and ye floods,
   And windy waves of woods;
Ye valleys and wild vineyards, ye lit lakes
   And happier hillside brakes,
Untrampled by the accursed feet that trod
   Fields golden from their god,
Fields of their god forsaken, whereof none
   Sees his face in the sun,
Hears his voice from the floweriest wildernesses;
   And, barren of his tresses,
Ye bays unplucked and laurels unentwined,
   That no men break or bind,
And myrtles long forgetful of the sword,
   And olives unadored,
Wisdom and love, white hands that save and slay,
   Praise him; and ye as they,
Praise him, O gracious might of dews and rains
   That feed the purple plains,
O sacred sunbeams bright as bare steel drawn,
   O cloud and fire and dawn;
Red hills of flame, white Alps, green Apennines,
   Banners of blowing pines,

Standards of stormy snows, flags of light leaves,
  Three wherewith Freedom weaves
One ensign that once woven and once unfurled
  Makes day of all a world,
Makes blind their eyes who knew not, and outbraves
  The waste of iron waves;
Ye fields of yellow fullness, ye fresh fountains,
  And mists of many mountains;
Ye moons and seasons, and ye days and nights;
  Ye starry-headed heights,
And gorges melting sunward from the snow,
  And all strong streams that flow,
Tender as tears, and fair as faith, and pure
  As hearts made sad and sure
At once by many sufferings and one love;
  O mystic deathless dove
Held to the heart of earth and in her hands
  Cherished, O lily of lands,
White rose of time, dear dream of praises past—
  For such as these thou wast,
That art as eagles setting to the sun,
  As fawns that leap and run,
As a sword carven with keen floral gold,
  Sword for an armed god's hold,
Flower for a crowned god's forehead—O our land,
  Reach forth thine holiest hand,
O mother of many sons and memories,
  Stretch out thine hand to his
That raised and gave thee life to run and leap
  When thou wast full of sleep,

That touched and stung thee with young blood and
    breath
When thou wast hard on death.
Praise him, O all her cities and her crowns,
    Her towers and thrones of towns;
O noblest Brescia, scarred from foot to head
    And breast-deep in the dead,
Praise him from all the glories of thy graves
    That yellow Mela laves
With gentle and golden water, whose fair flood
    Ran wider with thy blood:
Praise him, O born of that heroic breast,
    O nursed thereat and blest,
Verona, fairer than thy mother fair,
    But not more brave to bear:
Praise him, O Milan, whose imperial tread
    Bruised once the German head;
Whose might, by northern swords left desolate,
    Set foot on fear and fate:
Praise him, O long mute mouth of melodies,
    Mantua, with louder keys,
With mightier chords of music even than rolled
    From the large harps of old,
When thy sweet singer of golden throat and tongue,
    Praising his tyrant, sung;
Though now thou sing not as of other days,
    Learn late a better praise.
Not with the sick sweet lips of slaves that sing,
    Praise thou no priest or king,
No brow-bound laurel of discoloured leaf,
    But him, the crownless chief.

Praise him, O star of sun-forgotten times,
    Among their creeds and crimes
That wast a fire of witness in the night,
    Padua, the wise men's light :
Praise him, O sacred Venice, and the sea
    That now exults through thee,
Full of the mighty morning and the sun,
    Free of things dead and done ;
Praise him from all the years of thy great grief,
    That shook thee like a leaf
With winds and snows of torment, rain that fell
    Red as the rains of hell,
Storms of black thunder and of yellow flame,
    And all ill things but shame ;
Praise him with all thy holy heart and strength ;
    Through thy walls' breadth and length
Praise him with all thy people, that their voice
    Bid the strong soul rejoice,
The fair clear supreme spirit beyond stain,
    Pure as the depth of pain,
High as the head of suffering, and secure
    As all things that endure.
More than thy blind lord of an hundred years
    Whose name our memory hears,
Home-bound from harbours of the Byzantine
    Made tributary of thine,
Praise him who gave no gifts from oversea,
    But gave thyself to thee.
O mother Genoa, through all years that run,
    More than that other son,

Who first beyond the seals of sunset prest
  Even to the unfooted west,
Whose back-blown flag scared from their sheltering
      seas
  The unknown Atlantides,
And as flame climbs through cloud and vapour clomb
  Through streams of storm and foam,
Till half in sight they saw land heave and swim—
  More than this man praise him.
One found a world new-born from virgin sea ;
  And one found Italy.
O heavenliest Florence, from the mouths of flowers
  Fed by melodious hours,
From each sweet mouth that kisses light and air,
  Thou whom thy fate made fair,
As a bound vine or any flowering tree,
  Praise him who made thee free.
For no grape-gatherers trampling out the wine
  Tread thee, the fairest vine ;
For no man binds thee, no man bruises, none
  Does with thee as these have done.
From where spring hears loud through her long lit
      vales
  Triumphant nightingales,
In many a fold of fiery foliage hidden,
  Withheld as things forbidden,
But clamorous with innumerable delight
  In May's red, green, and white,
In the far-floated standard of the spring,
  That bids men also sing,

Our flower of flags, our witness that we are free,
  Our lamp for land and sea;
From where Majano feels through corn and vine
  Spring move and melt as wine,
And Fiesole's embracing arms enclose
  The immeasurable rose;
From hill-sides plumed with pine, and heights wind-worn
  That feel the refluent morn,
Or where the moon's face warm and passionate
  Burns, and men's hearts grow great,
And the swoln eyelids labour with sweet tears,
  And in their burning ears
Sound throbs like flame, and in their eyes new light
  Kindles the trembling night;
From faint illumined fields and starry valleys
  Wherefrom the hill-wind sallies,
From Vallombrosa, from Valdarno raise
  One Tuscan tune of praise.
O lordly city of the field of death,
  Praise him with equal breath,
From sleeping streets and gardens, and the stream
  That threads them as a dream
Threads without light the untravelled ways of sleep
  With eyes that smile or weep;
From the sweet sombre beauty of wave and wall
  That fades and does not fall;
From coloured domes and cloisters fair with fame,
  Praise thou and thine his name.
Thou too, O little laurelled town of towers,
  Clothed with the flame of flowers,

From windy ramparts girdled with young gold,
  From thy sweet hill-side fold
Of wallflowers and the acacia's belted bloom
  And every blowing plume,
Halls that saw Dante speaking, chapels fair
  As the outer hills and air,
Praise him who feeds the fire that Dante fed,
  Our highest heroic head,
Whose eyes behold through floated cloud and flame
  The maiden face of fame
Like April's in Valdelsa ; fair as flowers,
  And patient as the hours ;
Sad with slow sense of time, and bright with faith
  That levels life and death ;
The final fame, that with a foot sublime
  Treads down reluctant time ;
The fame that waits and watches and is wise,
  A virgin with chaste eyes,
A goddess who takes hands with great men's grief ;
  Praise her, and him, our chief.
Praise him, O Siena, and thou her deep green spring,
  O Fonte Branda, sing :
Shout from the red clefts of thy fiery crags,
  Shake out thy flying flags
In the long wind that streams from hill to hill ;
  Bid thy full music fill
The desolate red waste of sunset air
  And fields the old time saw fair,
But now the hours ring void through ruined lands,
  Wild work of mortal hands ;

Yet through thy dead Maremma let his name
  Take flight and pass in flame,
And the red ruin of disastrous hours
  Shall quicken into flowers.
Praise him, O fiery child of sun and sea,
  Naples, who bade thee be ;
For till he sent the swords that scourge and save,
  Thou wast not, but thy grave.
But more than all these praise him and give thanks,
  Thou, from thy Tiber's banks,
From all thine hills and from thy supreme dome,
  Praise him, O risen Rome.
Let all thy children cities at thy knee
  Lift up their voice with thee,
Saying ' for thy love's sake and our perished grief
  We laud thee, O our chief ; '
Saying ' for thine hand and help when hope was
    dead
  We thank thee, O our head ; '
Saying ' for thy voice and face within our sight
  We bless thee, O our light ;
For waters cleansing us from days defiled
  We praise thee, O our child.'

So with an hundred cities' mouths in one
  Praising thy supreme son,
Son of thy sorrow, O mother, O maid and mother,
  Our queen, who serve none other,
Our lady of pity and mercy, and full of grace,
  Turn otherwhere thy face,

Turn for a little and look what things are these
  Now fallen before thy knees ;
Turn upon them thine eyes who hated thee,
  Behold what things they be,
Italia : these are stubble that were steel,
  Dust, or a turning wheel ;
As leaves, as snow, as sand, that were so strong ;
  And howl, for all their song,
And wail, for all their wisdom ; they that were
  So great, they are all stript bare,
They are all made empty of beauty, and all abhorred ;
  They are shivered, and their sword ;
They are slain who slew, they are heartless who were
    wise ;
  Yea, turn on these thine eyes,
O thou, soliciting with soul sublime
  The obscure soul of time,
Thou, with the wounds thy holy body bears
  From broken swords of theirs,
Thou, with the sweet swoln eyelids that have bled
  Tears for thy thousands dead,
And upon these, whose swords drank up like dew
  The sons of thine they slew,
These, whose each gun blasted with murdering mouth
  Live flowers of thy fair south,
These, whose least evil told in alien ears
  Turned men's whole blood to tears,
These, whose least sin remembered for pure shame
  Turned all those tears to flame,

Even upon these, when breaks the extreme blow
  And all the world cries woe,
When heaven reluctant rains long-suffering fire
  On these and their desire,
When his wind shakes them and his waters whelm
  Who rent thy robe and realm,
When they that poured thy dear blood forth as wine
  Pour forth their own for thine,
On these, on these have mercy : not in hate,
  But full of sacred fate,
Strong from the shrine and splendid from the god,
  Smite, with no second rod.
Because they spared not, do thou rather spare :
  Be not one thing they were.
Let not one tongue of theirs who hate thee say
  That thou wast even as they.
Because their hands were bloody, be thine white ;
  Show light where they shed night :
Because they are foul, be thou the rather pure ;
  Because they are feeble, endure ;
Because they had no pity, have thou pity.

  And thou, O supreme city,
O priestless Rome that shalt be, take in trust
  Their names, their deeds, their dust,
Who held life less than thou wert ; be the least
  To thee indeed a priest,
Priest and burnt-offering and blood-sacrifice
  Given without prayer or price,
A holier immolation than men wist,
  A costlier eucharist,

A sacrament more saving ; bend thine head
 Above these many dead
Once, and salute with thine eternal eyes
 Their lowest head that lies.
Speak from thy lips of immemorial speech
 If but one word for each.
Kiss but one kiss on each thy dead son's mouth
 Fallen dumb or north or south.
And laying but once thine hand on brow and breast,
 Bless them, through whom thou art blest.
And saying in ears of these thy dead ' Well done,'
 Shall they not hear ' O son ' ?
And bowing thy face to theirs made pale for thee,
 Shall the shut eyes not see ?
Yea, through the hollow-hearted world of death,
 As light, as blood, as breath,
Shall there not flash and flow the fiery sense,
 The pulse of prescience ?
Shall not these know as in times overpast
 Thee loftiest to the last ?
For times and wars shall change, kingdoms and creeds,
 And dreams of men, and deeds ;
Earth shall grow grey with all her golden things,
 Pale peoples and hoar kings ;
But though her thrones and towers of nations fall,
 Death has no part in all ;.
In the air, nor in the imperishable sea,
 Nor heaven, nor truth, nor thee.
Yea, let all sceptre-stricken nations lie,
 But live thou though they die ;

Let their flags fade as flowers that storm can mar,
  But thine be like a star ;
Let England's, if it float not for men free,
  Fall, and forget the sea ;
Let France's, if it shadow a hateful head,
  Drop as a leaf drops dead ;
Thine let what storm soever smite the rest
  Smite as it seems him best ;
Thine let the wind that can, by sea or land,
  Wrest from thy banner-hand.
Die they in whom dies freedom, die and cease,
  Though the world weep for these ;
Live thou and love and lift when these lie dead
  The green and white and red.

O our Republic that shalt bind in bands
  The kingdomless far lands
And link the chainless ages ; thou that wast
  With England ere she past
Among the faded nations, and shalt be
  Again, when sea to sea
Calls through the wind and light of morning time,
  And throneless clime to clime
Makes antiphonal answer ; thou that art
  Where one man's perfect heart
Burns, one man's brow is brightened for thy sake,
  Thine, strong to make or break ;
O fair Republic hallowing with stretched hands
  The limitless free lands,

When all men's heads for love, not fear, bow down
    To thy sole royal crown,
As thou to freedom ; when man's life smells sweet,
    And at thy bright swift feet
A bloodless and a bondless world is laid ;
    Then, when thy men are made,
Let these indeed as we in dreams behold
    One chosen of all thy fold,
One of all fair things fairest, one exalt
    Above all fear or fault,
One unforgetful of unhappier men
    And us who loved her then ;
With eyes that outlook suns and dream on graves ;
    With voice like quiring waves ;
With heart the holier for their memories' sake
    Who slept that she might wake ;
With breast the sweeter for that sweet blood lost,
    And all the milkless cost ;
Lady of earth, whose large equality
    Bends but to her and thee ;
Equal with heaven, and infinite of years,
    And splendid from quenched tears ;
Strong with old strength of great things fallen and fled,
    Diviner for her dead ;
Chaste of all stains and perfect from all scars,
    Above all storms and stars,
All winds that blow through time, all waves that foam,
    Our Capitolian Rome.

1867.

D

ODE

ON THE

PROCLAMATION

OF THE

FRENCH REPUBLIC,

SEPTEMBER 4TH, 1870.

À VICTOR HUGO.

αἴλινον αἴλινον εἰπὲ, τὸ δ' εὖ νικάτω.

.

ODE ON THE PROCLAMATION OF THE FRENCH REPUBLIC.

STROPHE I.

WITH songs and crying and sounds of acclamations,
  Lo, the flame risen, the fire that falls in showers!
Hark; for the word is out among the nations:
  Look; for the light is up upon the hours:
O fears, O shames, O many tribulations,
  Yours were all yesterdays, but this day ours.
Strong were your bonds linked fast with lamentations,
  With groans and tears built into walls and towers;
Strong were your works and wonders of high stations,
  Your forts blood-based, and rampires of your powers:
Lo now the last of divers desolations,
  The hand of time, that gathers hosts like flowers;
Time, that fills up and pours out generations;
  Time, at whose breath confounded empire cowers.

STR. 2.

What are these moving in the dawn's red gloom?
What is she waited on by dread and doom,
Ill ministers of morning, bondsmen born of night?
  If that head veiled and bowed be morning's head,
  If she come walking between doom and dread,
Who shall rise up with song and dance before her sight?

Are not the night's dead heaped about her feet?
Is not death swollen, and slaughter full of meat?
What, is their feast a bride-feast, where men sing and
    dance?
A bitter, a bitter bride-song and a shrill
Should the house raise that such bride-followers fill,
Wherein defeat weds ruin, and takes for bride-bed
    France.

For nineteen years deep shame and sore desire
Fed from men's hearts with hungering fangs of fire,
And hope fell sick with famine for the food of change.
Now is change come, but bringing funeral urns;
Now is day nigh, but the dawn blinds and burns;
Now time long dumb hath language, but the tongue is
    strange.

We that have seen her not our whole lives long,
We to whose ears her dirge was cradle-song,
The dirge men sang who laid in earth her living head,
Is it by such light that we live to see
Rise, with rent hair and raiment, Liberty?
Does her grave open only to restore her dead?

Ah, was it this we looked for, looked and prayed,
This hour that treads upon the prayers we made,
This ravening hour that breaks down good and ill
    alike?
Ah, was it thus we thought to see her and hear,
The one love indivisible and dear?
Is it her head that hands which strike down wrong
    must strike?

STR. 3.

Where is hope, and promise where, in all these things,
Shocks of strength with strength, and jar of hurtling
    kings?
Who of all men, who will show us any good?
Shall these lightnings of blind battles give men light?
Where is freedom? who will bring us in her sight,
    That have hardly seen her footprint where she stood?

STR. 4.

Who is this that rises red with wounds and splendid,
    All her breast and brow made beautiful with scars,
Burning bare as naked daylight, undefended,
    In her hands for spoils her splintered prison-bars,
In her eyes the light and fire of long pain ended,
    In her lips a song as of the morning stars?

STR. 5.

O torn out of thy trance,
O deathless, O my France,
O many-wounded mother, O redeemed to reign!
O rarely sweet and bitter
The bright brief tears that glitter
On thine unclosing eyelids, proud of their own pain;
The beautiful brief tears
That wash the stains of years

White as the names immortal of thy chosen and slain.
  O loved so much so long,
  O smitten with such wrong,
O purged at last and perfect without spot or stain,
  Light of the light of man,
  Reborn republican,
At last, O first Republic, hailed in heaven again !
  Out of the obscene eclipse
  Re-risen, with burning lips
To witness for us if we looked for thee in vain.

STR. 6.

Thou wast the light whereby men saw
Light, thou the trumpet of the law
  Proclaiming manhood to mankind;
  And what if all these years were blind
And shameful ?   Hath the sun a flaw
Because one hour hath power to draw
  Mist round him wreathed as links to bind ?
And what if now keen anguish drains
The very wellspring of thy veins
  And very spirit of thy breath ?
The life outlives them and disdains ;
The sense which makes the soul remains,
  And blood of thought which travaileth
To bring forth hope with procreant pains.
O thou that satest bound in chains
Between thine hills and pleasant plains
  As whom his own soul vanquisheth,

Held in the bonds of his own thought,
Whence very death can take off nought,
Nor sleep, with bitterer dreams than death,—
What though thy thousands at thy knees
Lie thick as grave-worms feed on these,
Though thy green fields and joyous places
Are populous with blood-blackening faces
And wan limbs eaten by the sun?
Better an end of all men's races,
Better the world's whole work were done,
And life wiped out of all our traces,
And there were left to time not one,
Than such as these that fill thy graves
Should sow in slaves the seed of slaves.

ANTISTROPHE I.

Not of thy sons, O mother many-wounded,
Not of thy sons are slaves ingraffed and grown.
Was it not thine, the fire whence light rebounded
From kingdom on rekindling kingdom thrown,
From hearts confirmed on tyrannies confounded,
From earth on heaven, fire mightier than his own?
Not thine the breath wherewith time's clarion sounded,
And all the terror in the trumpet blown?
The voice whereat the thunders stood astounded
As at a new sound of a God unknown?
And all the seas and shores within them bounded
Shook at the strange speech of thy lips alone,
And all the hills of heaven, the storm-surrounded,
Trembled, and all the night sent forth a groan.

ANT. 2.

What hast thou done that such an hour should be
   More than another clothed with blood to thee?
Thou hast seen many a bloodred hour before this one.
   What art thou that thy lovers should misdoubt?
   What is this hour that it should cast hope out?
If hope turn back and fall from thee, what hast thou
      done?

Thou hast done ill against thine own soul; yea,
   Thine own soul hast thou slain and burnt away,
Dissolving it with poison into foul thin fume.
   Thine own life and creation of thy fate
   Thou hast set thine hand to unmake and discreate;
And now thy slain soul rises between dread and doom.

Yea, this is she that comes between them led;
   That veiled head is thine own soul's buried head,
The head that was as morning's in the whole world's
      sight.
   These wounds are deadly on thee, but deadlier
   Those wounds the ravenous poison left on her;
How shall her weak hands hold thy weak hands up to
      fight?

Ah, but her fiery eyes, her eyes are these
   That, gazing, make thee shiver to the knees
And the blood leap within thee, and the strong joy rise.

What, doth her sight yet make thine heart to dance?
O France, O freedom, O the soul of France,
Are ye then quickened, gazing in each other's eyes?

Ah, and her words, the words wherewith she sought
     thee
Sorrowing, and bare in hand the robe she wrought
     thee
To wear when soul and body were again made one,
And fairest among women, and a bride,
Sweet-voiced to sing the bridegroom to her side,
The spirit of man, the bridegroom brighter than the
     sun!

ANT. 3.

Who shall help me? who shall take me by the hand?
Who shall teach mine eyes to see, my feet to stand,
     Now my foes have stripped and wounded me by
          night?
Who shall heal me? who shall come to take my part?
Who shall set me as a seal upon his heart,
     As a seal upon his arm made bare for fight?

ANT. 4.

If thou know not, O thou fairest among women,
     If thou see not where the signs of him abide,
Lift thine eyes up to the light that stars grow dim in,
     To the morning whence he comes to take thy side.
None but he can bear the light that love wraps him in,
     When he comes on earth to take himself a bride.

ANT. 5.

Light of light, name of names,
Whose shadows are live flames,
The soul that moves the wings of worlds upon their
way ;
Life, spirit, blood and breath
In time and change and death
Substant through strength and weakness, ardour and
decay ;
Lord of the lives of lands,
Spirit of man, whose hands
Weave the web through wherein man's centuries fall
as prey ;
That art within our will
Power to make, save, and kill,
Knowledge and choice, to take extremities and weigh ;
In the soul's hand to smite
Strength, in the soul's eye sight ;
That to the soul art even as is the soul to clay ;
Now to this people be
Love ; come, to set them free,
With feet that tread the night, with eyes that sound
the day.

ANT. 6.

Thou that wast on their fathers dead
As effluent God effused and shed,

Heaven to be handled, hope made flesh,
Break for them now time's iron mesh;
Give them thyself for hand and head,
Thy breath for life, thy love for bread,
    Thy thought for spirit to refresh,
Thy bitterness to pierce and sting,
Thy sweetness for a healing spring.
    Be to them knowledge, strength, life, light,
Thou to whose feet the centuries cling
And in the wide warmth of thy wing
    Seek room and rest as birds by night,
O thou the kingless people's king,
To whom the lips of silence sing,
    Called by thy name of thanksgiving
    Freedom, and by thy name of might
Justice, and by thy secret name
Love; the same need is on the same
    Men, be the same God in their sight!
From this their hour of bloody tears
Their praise goes up into thine ears,
Their bruised lips clothe thy name with praises,
The song of thee their crushed voice raises,
    Their grief seeks joy for psalms to borrow,
With tired feet seeks her through time's mazes
    Where each day's blood leaves pale the morrow,
And from their eyes in thine there gazes
    A spirit other far than sorrow—
A soul triumphal, white and whole
And single, that salutes thy soul.

All the lights of the sweet heaven that sing together;
  All the years of the green earth that bare man free;
Rays and lightnings of the fierce or tender weather,
  Heights and lowlands, wastes and headlands of the
      sea,
Dawns and sunsets, hours that hold the world in tether,
  Be our witnesses and seals of things to be.
Lo the mother, the Republic universal,
  Hands that hold time fast, hands feeding men with
      might,
Lips that sing the song of the earth, that make rehearsal
  Of all seasons, and the sway of day with night,
Eyes that see as from a mountain the dispersal,
  The huge ruin of things evil, and the flight;
Large exulting limbs, and bosom godlike moulded
  Where the man-child hangs, and womb wherein he
      lay;
Very life that could it die would leave the soul dead,
  Face whereat all fears and forces flee away,
Breath that moves the world as winds a flower-bell
      folded,
  Feet that trampling the gross darkness beat out day.
      In the hour of pain and pity,
      Sore spent, a wounded city,
Her foster-child seeks to her, stately where she stands;
      In the utter hour of woes,
      Wind-shaken, blind with blows,
Paris lays hold upon her, grasps her with child's hands;

Face kindles face with fire,
Hearts take and give desire,
Strange joy breaks red as tempest on tormented lands.
Day to day, man to man,
Plights love republican,
And faith and memory burn with passion toward each
other;
Hope, with fresh heavens to track,
Looks for a breath's space back,
Where the divine past years reach hands to this their
brother;
And souls of men whose death
Was light to her and breath
Send word of love yet living to the living mother.
They call her, and she hears ;
O France, thy marvellous years,
The years of the strong travail, the triumphant time,
Days terrible with love,
Red-shod with flames thereof,
Call to this hour that breaks in pieces crown and crime ;
The hour with feet to spurn,
Hands to crush, fires to burn
The state whereto no latter foot of man shall climb.
Yea, come what grief now may
By ruinous night or day,
One grief there cannot, one the first and last grief,
shame.
Come force to break thee and bow
Down, shame can come not now,

E

Nor, though hands wound thee, tongues make mockery
　　of thy name :
　　　　Come swords and scar thy brow,
　　　　No brand there burns it now,
No spot but of thy blood marks thy white-fronted
　　fame.
　　　　Now though the mad blind morrow
　　　　With shafts of iron sorrow
Should split thine heart, and whelm thine head with
　　sanguine waves ;
　　　　Though all that draw thy breath
　　　　Bled from all veins to death,
And thy dead body were the grave of all their graves,
　　　　And thine unchilded womb
　　　　For all their tombs a tomb,
At least within thee as on thee room were none for
　　slaves.
　　　　This power thou hast, to be,
　　　　Come death or come not, free ;
That in all tongues of time's this praise be chanted of
　　thee,
　　　　That in thy wild worst hour
　　　　This power put in thee power,
And moved as hope around and hung as heaven above
　　thee,
　　　　And while earth sat in sadness
　　　　In only thee put gladness,
Put strength and love, to make all hearts of ages love
　　thee.

That in death's face thy chant
Arose up jubilant,
And thy great heart with thy great peril grew more
great :
And sweet for bitter tears
Put out the fires of fears,
And love made lovely for thee loveless hell and hate ;
And they that house with error,
Cold shame and burning terror,
Fled from truth risen and thee made mightier than thy
fate.
This shall all years remember ;
For this thing shall September
Have only name of honour, only sign of white.
And this year's fearful name,
France, in thine house of fame
Above all names of all thy triumphs shalt thou write,
When, seeing thy freedom stand
Even at despair's right hand,
The cry thou gavest at heart was only of delight.

DIRÆ.

Guai a voi, anime prave.

DANTE.

Soyez maudits, d'abord d'être ce que vous êtes,
Et puis soyez maudits d'obséder les poëtes !

VICTOR HUGO.

I.

A DEAD KING.

[Ferdinand II. entered Malebolge May 22nd, 1859.]

Go down to hell. This end is good to see ;
　The breath is lightened and the sense at ease
　Because thou art not ; sense nor breath there is
In what thy body was, whose soul shall be
Chief nerve of hell's pained heart eternally.
　Thou art abolished from the midst of these
　That are what thou wast : Pius from his knees
Blows off the dust that flecked them, bowed for thee.
Yea, now the long-tongued slack-lipped litanies
　Fail, and the priest has no more prayer to sell—·
Now the last Jesuit found about thee is
　The beast that made thy fouler flesh his cell—
Time lays his finger on thee, saying, ' Cease ;
　Here is no room for thee ; go down to hell.'

II.

A YEAR AFTER.

If blood throbs yet in this that was thy face,
  O thou whose soul was full of devil's faith,
  If in thy flesh the worm's bite slackeneth
In some acute red pause of iron days,
Arise now, gird thee, get thee on thy ways,
    Breathe off the worm that crawls and fears not
        breath ;
    King, it may be thou shalt prevail on death ;
King, it may be thy soul shall find out grace.
O spirit that hast eased the place of Cain,
    Weep now and howl, yea weep now sore ; for this
    That was thy kingdom hath spat out its king.
Wilt thou plead now with God ? behold again,
    Thy prayer for thy son's sake is turned to a hiss,
    Thy mouth to a snake's whose slime outlives the
        sting.

III.

PETER'S PENCE FROM PERUGIA.

ISCARIOT, thou grey-grown beast of blood,
  Stand forth to plead ; stand, while red drops run
    here
And there down fingers shaken with foul fear,
Down the sick shivering chin that stooped and sued,
Bowed to the bosom, for a little food
  At Herod's hand, who smites thee cheek and ear.
  Cry out, Iscariot ; haply he will hear ;
Cry, till he turn again to do thee good.
Gather thy gold up, Judas, all thy gold,
  · And buy thee death ; no Christ is here to sell,
But the dead earth of poor men bought and sold,
  While year heaps year above thee safe in hell,
To grime thy grey dishonourable head
With dusty shame, when thou art damned and dead.

IV.

PAPAL ALLOCUTION.

'Populc mi, quid tibi feci?'

WHAT hast thou done?   Hark, till thine ears wax hot,
  Judas ; for these and these things hast thou done.
    Thou hast made earth faint, and sickened the sweet
        sun,
With fume of blood that reeks from limbs that rot;
Thou hast washed thine hands and mouth, saying, ' Am
        I not
    Clean?' and thy lips were bloody, and there was
        none
    To speak for man against thee, no, not one ;
This hast thou done to us, Iscariot.
Therefore, though thou be deaf and heaven be dumb,
  A cry shall be from under to proclaim
    In the ears of all who shed men's blood or sell
Pius the Ninth, Judas the Second, come
  Where Boniface out of the filth and flame
    Barks for his advent in the clefts of hell.*

* Dante, ' Inferno,' xix. 53.

V.

THE BURDEN OF AUSTRIA.

1866.

O DAUGHTER of pride, wasted with misery,
　With all the glory that thy shame put on
　Stripped off thy shame, O daughter of Babylon,
Yea, whoso be it, yea, happy shall he be
That as thou hast served us hath rewarded thee.
　Blessed, who throweth against war's boundary stone
　Thy warrior brood, and breaketh bone by bone
Misrule thy son, thy daughter Tyranny.
That landmark shalt thou not remove for shame,
　But sitting down there in a widow's weed
Wail; for what fruit is now of thy red fame?
　Have thy sons too and daughters learnt indeed
　What thing it is to weep, what thing to bleed?
Is it not thou that now art but a name? *

* 'A geographical expression.'—Metternich of Italy.

VI

LOCUSTA.

COME close and see her and hearken.   This is she.
  Stop the ways fast against the stench that nips
  Your nostril as it nears her.   Lo, the lips
That between prayer and prayer find time to be
Poisonous, the hands holding a cup and key,
    Key of deep hell, cup whence blood reeks and
      drips ;
    The loose lewd limbs, the reeling hingeless hips,
The scurf that is not skin but leprosy.
This haggard harlot grey of face and green
    With the old hand's cunning mixes her new priest
      The cup she mixed her Nero, stirred and spiced.
She lisps of Mary and Jesus Nazarene
    With a tongue tuned, and head that bends to the
      east,
      Praying.   There are who say she is bride of
        Christ.

VII.

CELÆNO.

THE blind king hides his weeping eyeless head,
  Sick with the helpless hate and shame and awe,
  Till food have choked the glutted hell-bird's craw
And the foul cropful creature lie as dead
And soil itself with sleep and too much bread:
  So the man's life serves under the beast's law,
  And things whose spirit lives in mouth and maw
Share shrieking the soul's board and soil her bed,
Till man's blind spirit, their sick slave, resign
Its kingdom to the priests whose souls are swine,
  And the scourged serf lie reddening from their rod,
Discrowned, disrobed, dismantled, with lost eyes
Seeking where lurks in what conjectural skies
  That triple-headed hound of hell their God.

VIII.

A CHOICE.

FAITH is the spirit that makes man's body and blood
  Sacred, to crown when life and death have ceased
  His heavenward head for high fame's holy feast ;
But as one swordstroke swift as wizard's rod
Made Cæsar carrion and made Brutus God,
  Faith false or true, born patriot or born priest,
  Smites into semblance or of man or beast
The soul that feeds on clean or unclean food.
Lo here the faith that lives on its own light,
  Visible music ; and lo there, the foul
  Shape without shape, the harpy throat and howl.
Sword of the spirit of man ! arise and smite,
  And sheer through throat and claw and maw and
    tongue
  Kill the beast faith that lives on its own dung.

IX.

THE AUGURS.

LAY the corpse out on the altar ; bid the elect
  Slaves clear the ways of service spiritual,
  Sweep clean the stalled soul's serviceable stall,
Ere the chief priest's dismantling hands detect
The ulcerous flesh of faith all scaled and specked
  Beneath the bandages that hid it all,
  And with sharp edgetools œcumenical
The leprous carcases of creeds dissect.
As on the night ere Brutus grew divine
The sick-souled augurs found their ox or swine
  Heartless ; so now too by their after art
In the same Rome, at an uncleaner shrine,
  Limb from rank limb, and putrid part from part,
  They carve the corpse—a beast without a heart.

X.

A COUNSEL.

O STRONG Republic of the nobler years
   Whose white feet shine beside time's fairer flood
   That shall flow on the clearer for our blood
Now shed, and the less brackish for our tears ;
When time and truth have put out hopes and fears
   With certitude, and love has burst the bud,
     If these whose powers then down the wind shall
      scud
Still live to feel thee smite their eyes and ears,
When thy foot's tread hath crushed their crowns and
     creeds,
Care thou not then to crush the beast that bleeds,
   The snake whose belly cleaveth to the sod,
Nor set thine heel on men as on their deeds ;
   But let the worm Napoleon crawl untrod,
   Nor grant Mastai the gallows of his God.
         Pius IV

1869.

XI.

THE MODERATES.

Virtutem videant intabescantque relictâ.

SHE stood before her traitors bound and bare,
Clothed with her wounds and with her naked shame
As with a weed of fiery tears and flame,
Their mother-land, their common weal and care,
And they turned from her and denied, and sware
They did not know this woman nor her name.
And they took truce with tyrants and grew tame,
And gathered up cast crowns and creeds to wear,
And rags and shards regilded.   Then she took
In her bruised hands their broken pledge, and eyed
These men so late so loud upon her side
With one inevitable and tearless look,
That they might see her face whom they forsook ;
And they beheld what they had left, and died.

February, 1870.

XII.

INTERCESSION.

Ave Cæsar Imperator, moriturum te saluto.

I.

O DEATH, a little more, and then the worm ;
 A little longer, O Death, a little yet,
 Before the grave gape and the grave-worm fret ;
Before the sanguine-spotted hand infirm
Be rottenness, and that foul brain, the germ
 Of all ill things and thoughts, be stopped and set ;
 A little while, O Death, ere he forget,
A small space more of life, a little term ;
A little longer ere he and thou be met,
 Ere in that hand that fed thee to thy mind
The poison-cup of life be overset ;
 A little respite of disastrous breath,
 Till the soul lift up her lost eyes, and find
 Nor God nor help nor hope, but thee, O Death.

II.

Shall a man die before his dying day,
  Death? and for him though the utter day be nigh,
  Not yet, not yet we give him leave to die ;
We give him grace not yet that men should say
He is dead, wiped out, perished and past away.
  Till the last bitterness of life go by,
  Thou shalt not slay him ; till those last dregs run
      dry,
O thou last lord of life ! thou shalt not slay.
Let the lips live a little while and lie,
  The hand a little, and falter, and fail of strength,
And the soul shudder and sicken at the sky ;
  Yea, let him live, though God nor man would let
  Save for the curse' sake ; then at bitter length,
    Lord, will we yield him to thee, but not yet.

III.

Hath he not deeds to do and days to see
　　Yet ere the day that is to see him dead?
　　Beats there no brain yet in the poisonous head,
Throbs there no treason? if no such thing there be,
If no such thought, surely this is not he.
　　Look to the hands then ; are the hands not red?
　　What are the shadows about this man's bed?
Death, was not this the cupbearer to thee?
Nay, let him live then, till in this life's stead
　　Even he shall pray for that thou hast to give ;
Till seeing his hopes and not his memories fled
　　Even he shall cry upon thee a bitter cry,
　　That life is worse than death ; then let him live,
　　Till death seem worse than life ; then let him die.

IV.

O watcher at the guardless gate of kings,
  O doorkeeper that serving at their feast
  Hast in thine hand their doomsday drink, and seest
With eyeless sight the soul of unseen things ;
Thou in whose ear the dumb time coming sings,
  Death, priest and king that makest of king and
    priest
  A name, a dream, a less thing than the least,
Hover awhile above him with closed wings,
Till the coiled soul, an evil snake-shaped beast,
  Eat its base bodily lair of flesh away ;
If haply, or ever its cursed life have ceased,
  Or ever thy cold hands cover his head
  From sight of France and freedom and broad day,
He may see these and wither and be dead.

PARIS, *September*, 1869.

XIII.

THE SAVIOUR OF SOCIETY.

I.

O SON of man, but of what man who knows?
  That broughtest healing on thy leathern wings
  To priests, and under them didst gather kings,
And madest friends to thee of all man's foes;
Before thine incarnation, the tale goes,
  Thy virgin mother, pure of sensual stings,
  Communed by night with angels of chaste things,
And, full of grace, untimely felt the throes
Of motherhood upon her, and believed
  The obscure annunciation made when late
  A raven-feathered raven-throated dove
  Croaked salutation to the mother of love
Whose misconception was immaculate,
And when her time was come she misconceived.

II.

Thine incarnation was upon this wise,
   Saviour ; and out of east and west were led
   To thy foul cradle by thy planet red
Shepherds of souls that feed their sheep with lies
Till the utter soul die as the body dies,
   And the wise men that ask but to be fed
   Though the hot shambles be their board and bed
And sleep on any dunghill shut their eyes,
So they lie warm and fatten in the mire :
   And the high priest enthroned yet in thy name,
Judas, baptised thee with men's blood for hire ;
   And now thou hangest nailed to thine own shame
   In sight of all time, but while heaven has flame
Shalt find no resurrection from hell-fire.

December, 1869.

XIV.

MENTANA: SECOND ANNIVERSARY.

Est-ce qu'il n'est pas temps que la foudre se prouve,
Cieux profonds, en broyant ce chien, fils de la louve?
La Légende des Siècles :—Ratbert.

I.

By the dead body of Hope, the spotless lamb
  Thou threwest into the high priest's slaughtering-
    room,
  And by the child Despair born red therefrom
As, thank the secret sire picked out to cram
With spurious spawn thy misconceiving dam,
  Thou, like a worm from a town's common tomb,
  Didst creep from forth the kennel of her womb,
Born to break down with catapult and ram
Man's builded towers of promise, and with breath
And tongue to track and hunt his hopes to death :
  O, by that sweet dead body abused and slain,
And by that child mismothered,—dog, by all
Thy curses thou hast cursed mankind withal,
  With what curse shall man curse thee back again ?

By the brute soul that made man's soul its food ;
　By time grown poisonous with it ; by the hate
　And horror of all souls not miscreate ;
By the hour of power that evil hath on good ;
And by the incognizable fatherhood
　Which made a whorish womb the shameful gate
　That opening let out loose to fawn on fate
A hound half-blooded ravening for man's blood ;
(What prayer but this for thee should any say,
　Thou dog of hell, but this that Shakespeare said ?)
By night deflowered and desecrated day,
　That fall as one curse on one cursed head,
' Cancel his bond of life, dear God, I pray,
　That I may live to say, The dog is dead ! '

1869.

XV.

MENTANA: THIRD ANNIVERSARY.

I.

Such prayers last year were put up for thy sake ;
  What shall this year do that hath lived to see
  The piteous and unpitied end of thee ?
What moan, what cry, what clamour shall it make,
Seeing as a reed breaks all thine empire break,
  And all thy great strength as a rotten tree,
  Whose branches made broad night from sea to sea,
And the world shuddered when a leaf would shake ?
From the unknown deep wherein those prayers were
      heard,
From the dark height of time there sounds a word,
  Crying, Comfort ; though death ride on this red
      hour,
    Hope waits with eyes that make the morning dim,
  Till liberty, reclothed with love and power,
    Shall pass and know not if she tread on him.

II.

The hour for which men hungered and had thirst,
  And dying were loth to die before it came,
  Is it indeed upon thee? and the lame
Late foot of vengeance on thy trace accurst
For years insepulchred and crimes inhearsed,
  For days marked red or black with blood or shame,
  Hath it outrun thee to tread out thy name?
This scourge, this hour, is this indeéd the worst?
O clothed and crowned with curses, canst thou tell?
  Have thy dead whispered to thee what they see
  Whose eyes are open in the dark on thee
Ere spotted soul and body take farewell
  Or what of life beyond the worm's may be
Satiate the immitigable hours in hell?

1870.

XVI.

THE DESCENT INTO HELL.

January 9th, 1873.

I.

O NIGHT and death, to whom we grudged him then,
  When in man's sight he stood not yet undone,
  Your king, your priest, your saviour, and your son,
We grudge not now, who know that not again
Shall this curse come upon the sins of men,
  Nor this face look upon the living sun
  That shall behold not so abhorred an one
In all the days whereof his eye takes ken.
The bond is cancelled, and the prayer is heard
  That seemed so long but weak and wasted breath ;
  Take him, for he is yours, O night and death.
Hell yawns on him whose life was as a word
  Uttered by death in hate of heaven and light,
  A curse now dumb upon the lips of night.

II.

What shapes are these and shadows without end
  That fill the night full as a storm of rain
  With myriads of dead men and women slain,
Old with young, child with mother, friend with friend,
That on the deep mid wintering air impend,
  Pale yet with mortal wrath and human pain,
  Who died that this man dead now too might reign,
Toward whom their hands point and their faces bend?
The ruining flood would redden earth and air
  If for each soul whose guiltless blood was shed
  There fell but one drop on this one man's head
Whose soul to-night stands bodiless and bare,
For whom our hearts give thanks who put up prayer,
  That we have lived to say, The dog is dead.

XVI.

APOLOGIA.

If wrath embitter the sweet mouth of song,
    And make the sunlight fire before those eyes
    That would drink draughts of peace from the
        unsoiled skies,
The wrongdoing is not ours, but ours the wrong,
Who hear too loud on earth and see too long
    The grief that dies not with the groan that dies,
    Till the strong bitterness of pity cries
Within us, that our anger should be strong.
For chill is known by heat and heat by chill,
And the desire that hope makes love to still
    By the fear flying beside it or above,
    A falcon fledged to follow a fledgeling dove,
And by the fume and flame of hate of ill
    The exuberant light and burning bloom of love.

LONDON : PRINTED BY
SPOTTISWOODE AND CO., NEW-STREET SQUARE
AND PARLIAMENT STREET

A List of Books

PUBLISHED BY

CHATTO & WINDUS

74 & 75, *PICCADILLY, LONDON, W.*

ADVERTISING, A HISTORY OF, from the Earliest Times. Illustrated by Anecdotes, Curious Specimens, and Biographical Notes of Successful Advertisers. By HENRY SAMPSON. Crown 8vo, with Coloured Frontispiece and Illustrations, cloth gilt, 7s. 6d.

"Nowhere is humanity so frank and real as in the advertising columns of the journals. Mr. Sampson has contrived to give us much of the essence of these columns, and therefore of humanity as it really is. The chapters devoted to hoaxing advertisements and their results are exceedingly entertaining ; the author has also found a good deal that is pertinent to say of lotteries. On the whole, he has proved himself fairly equal to a comprehensive and difficult subject, and has produced a book that will be read with unflagging interest."—*Pall Mall Gazette.*

"We have here a book to be thankful for. Mr. Sampson carries us pretty well over the world to show us how wit, audacity, craft, and cunning have been employed in advertising. Among the many interesting illustrations to this book is a photographed copy of the *Times* for January 1st, 1788, which may be easily read by means of a magnifying glass. We recommend the present volume, which takes us through antiquity, the Middle Ages, and the present time, illustrating all in turn by advertisements—serious, comic, roguish, or downright rascally. The chapter on ' swindles and hoaxes' is full of entertainment ; but of that the volume itself is full from the first page to the last."—*Athenæum.*

ÆSOP'S FABLES TRANSLATED INTO HUMAN NATURE. By C. H. BENNETT. Crown 4to, 24 Plates beautifully printed in Colours, with descriptive Text, cloth extra, 6s.

" For fun and frolic the new version of Æsop's Fables must bear away the palm. There are twenty-two fables and twenty-two wonderful coloured illustrations ; the moral is pointed, the tale adorned. This is not a juvenile book, but there are plenty of grown-up children who like to be amused at Christmas, and indeed at any time of the year ; and if this new version of old stories does not amuse them they must be very dull indeed, and their situation one much to be commiserated."—*Morning Post.*

AINSWORTH'S LATIN DICTIONARY. The only Modern Edition which comprises the Complete Work. With numerous Additions, Emendations, and Improvements, by the Rev. B. W. BEATSON and W. ELLIS. Imperial 8vo, cloth extra, 15s.—Also, A SCHOOL EDITION, Revised and Corrected by Dr. JAMIESON. Containing all the Words of the Quarto Dictionary, but with a reduction in the number of Examples. Demy 8vo, roan, 9s.

AMUSING POETRY. A Selection of Humorous Verse from the Best Writers. Edited, with Preface, by SHIRLEY BROOKS. Fcap. 8vo, cloth, gilt edges, 3s. 6d.

ANACREON. Translated by THOMAS MOORE, and Illustrated by the exquisite Designs of GIRODET. Oblong 8vo, Etruscan gold and blue, 12s. 6d.

ARMY LISTS OF THE ROUNDHEADS AND CAVALIERS IN THE CIVIL WAR, 1642. SECOND EDITION, Corrected and considerably Enlarged. Edited, with Notes and full Index, by EDWARD PEACOCK, F.S.A. 4to, half-Roxburghe, 7s. 6d.

ARTEMUS WARD, COMPLETE.— The Works of CHARLES FARRER BROWNE, better known as ARTEMUS WARD. With fine Portrait, facsimile of Handwriting, &c. Crown 8vo, cloth extra, 7s. 6d.

ARTEMUS WARD'S LECTURE AT THE EGYPTIAN HALL, with the Panorama. Edited by T. W. ROBERTSON and E. P. HINGSTON. With numerous Illustrations. Small 4to, green and gold, 6s.

AS PRETTY AS SEVEN, and other Popular German Stories. Collected by LUDWIG BECHSTEIN. With Additional Tales by the Brothers GRIMM, and 100 Illustrations by RICHTER. Small 4to, green and gold, 6s. 6d. : gilt edges, 7s. 6d.

BACON'S (Francis, Lord) WORKS, both English and Latin, with an Introductory Essay, Biographical and Critical, and copious Indexes. Two Vols., imperial 8vo, with Portrait, cloth extra, £1 4s.

BARDSLEY'S ENGLISH SURNAMES : Their Sources and Significations. By CHARLES WAREING BARDSLEY, M.A. SECOND EDITION, revised throughout, considerably Enlarged, and partially rewritten. Crown 8vo, cloth extra, 9s.

"Mr. Bardsley has faithfully consulted the original mediæval documents and works from which the origin and development of surnames can alone be satisfactorily traced. He has furnished a valuable contribution to the literature of surnames, and we hope to hear more of him in this field."—*Times.*

BARLOW'S (George) UNDER THE DAWN. Crown 8vo, cloth extra, 7s. 6d.

BAUER AND HOOKER'S GENERA OF FERNS; in which the Characters of each Genus are displayed in a series of magnified dissections and figures, highly finished in colours, after the drawings of FRANCIS BAUER, with letterpress by Sir WILLIAM HOOKER. Imperial 8vo, with 120 beautifully Coloured Plates, half-morocco, gilt, £5 5s.

BAXTER'S (Richard) WORKS. With a Sketch of the Life and an Essay on the Genius of the Author. Four Vols., imperial 8vo, with Portrait, cloth extra, £2 8s.

BEAUTIFUL PICTURES BY BRITISH ARTISTS : A Gathering of Favourites from our Picture Galleries. In Two Series. The FIRST SERIES including Examples by WILKIE, CONSTABLE, TURNER, MULREADY, LANDSEER, MACLISE, E. M. WARD, FRITH, Sir JOHN GILBERT, LESLIE, ANSDELL, MARCUS STONE, Sir NOEL PATON, FAED, EYRE CROWE, GAVIN, O'NEIL, and MADOX BROWN. The SECOND containing Pictures by ARMYTAGE, FAED, GOODALL, HEMSLEY, HORSLEY, MARKS, NICHOLLS, Sir NOEL PATON, PICKERSGILL, G. SMITH, MARCUS STONE, SOLOMON, STRAIGHT, E. M. WARD, and WARREN. All engraved on Steel in the highest style of Art. Edited, with Notices of the Artists, by SYDNEY ARMYTAGE, M.A. Price of each Series, imperial 4to, cloth extra, gilt and gilt edges, 21s. *Each Volume is Complete in itself.*

BELL'S (Sir Charles) ANATOMY OF EXPRESSION, as
connected with the Fine Arts. Fifth Edition, with an Appendix on the Nervous
System by ALEXANDER SHAW. Illustrated with 45 beautiful Engravings. Imp.
8vo, cloth extra, gilt, 16s.

"The artist, the writer of fiction, the dramatist, the man of taste, will receive the
present work (which is got up with an elegance worthy of its subject) with gratitude,
and peruse it with a lively and increasing interest and delight."—*Christian Remem-
brancer.*

BINGHAM'S ANTIQUITIES of the CHRISTIAN CHURCH.
A New Edition, revised, with copious Index. Two Vols., imperial 8vo, cloth
extra, £1 4s.

" A writer who does equal honour to the English clergy and to the English nation,
and whose learning is to be equalled only by his moderation and impartiality."—
Quarterly Review.

**BIOGRAPHICAL AND CRITICAL DICTIONARY OF RE-
CENT AND LIVING PAINTERS AND ENGRAVERS,** both English and
Foreign. By HENRY OTTLEY. Being a Supplementary Volume to " Bryan's
Dictionary." Imperial 8vo, cloth extra, 12s.

*** *This is the only work giving an account of the principal living painters
of all countries.*

BLAKE'S WORKS.—A Series of Reproductions in Facsimile of the
Works of WILLIAM BLAKE, including the " Songs of Innocence and Experience,"
"The Book of Thel," "America," "The Vision of the Daughters of Albion,"
"The Marriage of Heaven and Hell," " Europe, a Prophecy," " Jerusalem,"
"Milton," " Urizen," " The Song of Los," &c. These Works will be issued both
coloured and plain.   [*In preparation.*

" Blake is a real name, I assure you, and a most extraordinary man he is, if he
still be living. He is the Blake whose wild designs accompany a splendid edition
of Blair's 'Grave.' He paints in water-colours marvellous strange pictures—
visions of his brain—which he asserts he has seen. They have great merit. I
must look upon him as one of the most extraordinary persons of the age."—CHARLES
LAMB.

BLANCHARD'S (Laman) POEMS. Now first Collected. Edited,
with a Life of the Author, and much interesting Correspondence, by BLANCHARD
JERROLD. Crown 8vo, cloth extra.   [*In preparation.*

BOCCACCIO'S DECAMERON; or, Ten Days' Entertainment.
Translated into English, with Introduction by THOMAS WRIGHT, Esq., M.A.,
F.S.A. With Portrait after RAPHAEL, and STOTHARD'S beautiful Copperplates.
Crown 8vo, cloth extra, gilt, 7s. 6d.

BOLTON'S SONG BIRDS OF GREAT BRITAIN. Illustrated
with Figures, the size of Life, of both Male and Female ; of their Nests and Eggs,
Food, Favourite Plants, Shrubs, Trees, &c. &c. Two Vols. in One, royal 4to,
containing 80 beautifully Coloured Plates, half-Roxburghe, £3 13s. 6d.

BOOK OF HALL MARKS; or, Manual of Reference for the
Goldsmith and Silversmith. By ALFRED LUTSCHAUNIG. Crown 8vo, with 46
Plates of the Hall-marks of the different Assay Towns of the United Kingdom.
7s. 6d.

BOOKSELLERS, A HISTORY OF. Including the Story of
the Rise and Progress of the Great Publishing Houses, in London and the
Provinces, and of their greatest Works. By HARRY CURWEN. Crown 8vo, with
Frontispiece and numerous Portraits and Illustrations, cloth extra, 7s. 6d.

"In these days, ten ordinary Histories of Kings and Courtiers were well ex-
changed against the tenth part of one good History of Booksellers."—THOMAS
CARLYLE.

"This stout little book is unquestionably amusing. Ill-starred, indeed, must be
the reader who, opening it anywhere, lights upon six consecutive pages within the
entire compass of which some good anecdote or smart repartee is not to be found."
—*Saturday Review.*

BOUDOIR BALLADS : Vers de Société. By J. Ashby Sterry.
Crown 8vo, cloth extra. [*In preparation.*

BRET HARTE'S CHOICE WORKS in Prose and Poetry. With
Introductory Essay by J. M. Bellew, Portrait of the Author, and 50 Illustrations. Crown 8vo, cloth extra, 7s. 6d.

BREWSTER'S (Sir David) MARTYRS OF SCIENCE. A
New Edition, in small crown 8vo, cloth extra, gilt, with full-page Portraits, 4s. 6d.

BREWSTER'S (Sir David) MORE WORLDS THAN ONE,
the Creed of the Philosopher and the Hope of the Christian. A New Edition, in small crown 8vo, cloth extra, gilt, with full-page Astronomical Plates, 4s. 6d.

BRIC-A-BRAC HUNTER (The) ; or, Chapters on Chinamania.
By Major H. Byng Hall. With Photographic Frontispiece, and numerous Illustrations. Crown 8vo, cloth extra, 10s. 6d. [*In the Press.*

BRIGHT'S (John, M.P.) SPEECHES on Public Affairs of the
last Twenty Years. Collated with the best Public Reports. Royal 16mo, 370 pages, cloth extra, 1s.

BRITISH ESSAYISTS (The) : viz., "Spectator," "Tatler,"
"Guardian," "Rambler," "Adventurer," "Idler," and "Connoisseur." Complete in Three thick Vols., 8vo, with Portrait, cloth extra, £1 7s.

BROADSTONE HALL, and other Poems. By W. E. Windus.
With 40 Illustrations by Alfred Concanen. Crown 8vo, cloth extra, gilt, 5s.

"This little volume of poems is illustrated with such vigour, and shows such a thoroughly practical knowledge of and love for sea-life, that it is quite tonic and refreshing. Maudlin sentimentality is carefully eschewed, and a robust, manly tone of thought gives muscle to the verse and elasticity of mind to the reader."—*Morning Post.*

BROCKEDON'S PASSES OF THE ALPS. Containing 109
fine Engravings by Finden, Willmore, and others ; with Maps of each Pass, and a General Map of the Alps by Arrowsmith. Two Vols., 4to, half-bound morocco, gilt edges, £3 13s. 6d.

BULWER'S (Lytton) PILGRIMS OF THE RHINE. With
Portrait and 27 exquisite Line Engravings on Steel, by Goodall, Willmore, and others ; after Drawings by David Roberts and Maclise. Crown 8vo, cloth extra, top edges gilt, 10s. 6d.

BUNYAN'S PILGRIM'S PROGRESS, With 17 beautiful Steel
Engravings by Stothard, engraved by Goodall ; and numerous Woodcuts. Square 8vo, cloth gilt, 10s. 6d.

BURNET'S HISTORY OF HIS OWN TIME, from the Restora-
tion of Charles II. to the Treaty of Peace at Utrecht. With Historical and Biographical Notes and copious Index. Imp. 8vo, with Portrait, cloth extra, 13s. 6d.

BURNET'S HISTORY OF THE REFORMATION OF THE
CHURCH OF ENGLAND. A New Edition, with numerous illustrative Notes and copious Index. Two Vols., imperial 8vo, cloth extra, £1 1s.

BYRON'S (Lord) LETTERS AND JOURNALS. With
Notices of his Life. By Thomas Moore. A Reprint of the Original Edition, newly revised, complete in a thick volume of 1060 pp., with Twelve full-page Plates. Crown 8vo, cloth extra, gilt, 7s. 6d.

"We have read this book with the greatest pleasure. Considered merely as a composition, it deserves to be classed among the best specimens of English prose which our age has produced. . . . The style is agreeable, clear, and manly, and, when it rises into eloquence, rises without effort or ostentation. Nor is the matter inferior to the manner. It would be difficult to name a book which exhibits more kindness, fairness, and modesty."—Macaulay, in the *Edinburgh Review.*

CALMET'S BIBLE DICTIONARY. Edited by CHARLES TAYLOR. With the Fragments incorporated and arranged in Alphabetical Order. New Edition. Imperial 8vo, with Maps and Wood Engravings, cloth extra, 10s. 6d.

CANOVA'S WORKS IN SCULPTURE AND MODELLING. 150 Plates exquisitely engraved in Outline by MOSES. With Descriptions by the Countess ALBRIZZI, and a Biographical Memoir by CICOGNARA. Three Vols., imperial 8vo, with Portrait by WORTHINGTON, half-Roxburghe, £2 5s.

CARLYLE (Thomas) ON THE CHOICE OF BOOKS. With New Life and Anecdotes. Small post 8vo, brown cloth, 1s. 6d.

CAROLS OF COCKAYNE ; Vers de Société descriptive of London Life. By HENRY S. LEIGH. Third Edition. With numerous Illustrations by ALFRED CONCANEN. Crown 8vo, cloth extra, gilt, 5s.

CARTER'S ANCIENT ARCHITECTURE OF ENGLAND. Including the Orders during the British, Roman, Saxon, and Norman Eras ; and also under the Reigns of Henry III. and Edward III. Illustrated by 103 large Copper-plate Engravings, comprising upwards of Two Thousand Specimens. Edited by JOHN BRITTON. Royal folio, half-morocco extra, £2 8s.

*** *This national work on ancient architecture occupied its author, in drawing, etching, arranging, and publishing, more than twenty years, and he himself declared it to be the result of his studies through life.*

CARTER'S ANCIENT SCULPTURE NOW REMAINING IN ENGLAND, from the Earliest Period to the Reign of Henry VIII.; consisting of Statues, Basso-relievos, Sculptures, &c., Brasses, Monumental Effigies, Paintings on Glass and on Walls ; Missal Ornaments ; Carvings on Cups, Croziers, Chests, Seals ; Ancient Furniture, &c. &c. With Historical and Critical Illustrations by DOUCE, MEYRICK, DAWSON TURNER, and JOHN BRITTON. Royal folio, with 120 large Engravings, many illuminated, half-bound morocco extra, £8 8s.

CATLIN'S ILLUSTRATIONS OF THE MANNERS, CUS-TOMS, AND CONDITION OF THE NORTH AMERICAN INDIANS, written during Eight Years of Travel and Adventure among the Wildest and most Remarkable Tribes now existing. Containing 360 Engravings from the Author's original Paintings. Tenth Edition. Two Vols., imperial 8vo, cloth extra, gilt, £1 10s.; or with the Plates beautifully Coloured, half-morocco, gilt edges, £8 8s.

"One of the most admirable observers of manners who ever lived among the aborigines of America."—*Humboldt's Cosmos.*

CATLIN'S NORTH AMERICAN INDIAN PORTFOLIO. Containing Hunting Scenes, Amusements, Scenery, and Costume of the Indians of the Rocky Mountains and Prairies of America, from Drawings and Notes made by the Author during Eight Years' Travel. A series of 25 magnificent Plates, beautifully coloured in facsimile of the Original Drawings exhibited at the Egyptian Hall. With letterpress descriptions, imp. folio, in handsome portfolio, £7 10s.

CELEBRATED CLAIMANTS, Ancient and Modern. The History of all the most celebrated Pretenders and Claimants, from PERKIN WARBECK to ARTHUR ORTON. Fcap. 8vo, illustrated boards, 2s.

CHAMBERLAINE'S IMITATIONS OF DRAWINGS FROM THE GREAT MASTERS in the Royal Collection. Engraved by BARTOLOZZI and others. 74 fine Plates, mostly tinted : including, in addition, "Ecce Homo," after GUIDO, and the scarce Series of 7 Anatomical Drawings. Imperial folio, half-morocco, gilt edges, £5 5s.

CHATTO'S (W. Andrew) HISTORY OF WOOD ENGRAVING, Historical and Practical. A New Edition, with an Additional Chapter. Illustrated by 445 fine Wood Engravings. Imperial 8vo, half-Roxburghe, £2 5s.

"This volume is one of the most interesting and valuable of modern times."—*Art Union.*

CHRISTMAS CAROLS AND BALLADS. Selected and
Edited by JOSHUA SYLVESTER. Cloth extra, gilt, gilt edges, 3s. 6d.

CICERO'S FAMILIAR LETTERS, AND LETTERS TO
ATTICUS. Translated by MELMOTH and HEBERDEN. With Life of Cicero by
MIDDLETON. Royal 8vo, with Portrait, cloth extra, 12s.

"Cicero is the type of a perfect letter-writer, never boring you with moral essays
out of season, always evincing his mastery over his art by the most careful con-
sideration for your patience and amusement. We should rifle the volumes of antiquity in vain to find a letter-writer who converses on paper so naturally, so
engagingly, so much from the heart, as Cicero."—*Quarterly Review.*

CLAUDE'S LIBER VERITATIS. A Collection of 303 Prints
after the Original Designs of CLAUDE. Engraved by RICHARD EARLOM. With
a descriptive Catalogue of each Print, Lists of the Persons for whom, and the Places
for which, the original Pictures were first painted, and of the present Possessors
of most of them. Three Vols. folio, half-morocco extra, gilt edges, £10 10s.

CLAUDE, BEAUTIES OF, containing 24 of his choicest Land-
scapes, beautifully Engraved on Steel, by BROMLEY, LUPTON, and others. With
Biographical Sketch and Portrait. Royal folio, in a portfolio, £1 5s.

COLLINS' (Wilkie) NOVELS. New Illustrated Library Editions,
price 6s. each, with Steel-plate Frontispiece, and several full-page Illustrations in
each Volume:—

The Woman in White.	Hide and Seek ; or, The Mys-
Antonina ; or, The Fall of Rome.	tery of Mary Grice.
	Man and Wife.
Basil.	Poor Miss Finch.
The Dead Secret.	Miss or Mrs. ?
The Queen of Hearts.	The New Magdalen.
The Moonstone.	The Frozen Deep.

MR. COLLINS' NEW NOVEL.

THE LAW AND THE LADY, in Three Vols., crown 8vo,
31s. 6d., is now ready at all Libraries and at the Booksellers.

"An exceedingly clever novel, full of admirable writing, abounding in a subtle
ingenuity which is a distinct order of genius. . . . . 'The Law and the Lady'
will be read with avidity by all who delight in the romances of the greatest master
the sensational novel has ever known."—*World.*

MY MISCELLANIES: Sketches and Essays by WILKIE COLLINS.
Two Vols., crown 8vo, 21s.   [*Shortly.*

COLMAN'S HUMOROUS WORKS.—Broad Grins, My Night-
gown and Slippers, and other Humorous Works, Prose and Poetical, of GEORGE
COLMAN. With Life and Anecdotes by G. B. BUCKSTONE, and Frontispiece by
HOGARTH. Crown 8vo, cloth extra, gilt, 7s. 6d.

CONDÉ (THE GREAT), and the Period of the Fronde : An
Historical Sketch. By WALTER FITZPATRICK. Second Edition. Two Vols.,
8vo, cloth extra, 15s.

CONQUEST OF THE SEA (The). A History of Diving
from the Earliest Times. By HENRY SIEBE. Profusely Illustrated. Crown 8vo,
cloth extra, gilt, 4s. 6d.

"We have perused this volume, full of quaint information, with delight. Mr.
Siebe has bestowed much pains on his work ; he writes with enthusiasm and fulness
of knowledge."—*Echo.*

"Really interesting alike to youths and to grown-up people."—*Scotsman.*

CONEY'S ENGRAVINGS OF ANCIENT CATHEDRALS,
Hôtels de Ville, Town Halls, &c., including some of the finest Examples of Gothic
Architecture in France, Holland, Germany, and Italy. 32 large Plates, imperial
folio, half-morocco extra, £3 13s. 6d.

CONSTABLE'S GRAPHIC WORKS. Comprising 40 highly
finished Mezzotinto Engravings on Steel, by DAVID LUCAS; with descriptive
Letterpress by C. R. LESLIE, R.A. Folio, half-morocco, gilt edges, £2 2s.

CORNWALL (PAROCHIAL HISTORY of the COUNTY of).
Compiled from the Best Authorities, and corrected and improved from Actual
Survey. Four Vols., 4to, cloth extra, £3 3s. the Set; or, separately, the first
Three Vols., 16s. each; the Fourth Vol., 18s.

* *With the Parochial History are embodied the writings of Hals and Tonkin.
The work also comprises the Itineraries of Leland and William of Worcester—
the Valor of Bishop Veysey—an Historical Account of the personal Campaign of
Charles I. in Cornwall during the "Great Rebellion," illustrated with letters,
diaries, and other interesting documents never before collected together—a complete Heraldry of the county—a larger list of Sheriffs than has hitherto been
published—Tales of the population, Domesday Manors, &c.*

COTMAN'S ENGRAVINGS OF THE SEPULCHRAL
BRASSES IN NORFOLK AND SUFFOLK. With Letterpress Descrip-
tions, an Essay on Sepulchral Memorials by DAWSON TURNER, Notes by Sir
SAMUEL MEYRICK, ALBERT WAY, and Sir HARRIS NICOLAS, and copious Index.
New Edition, containing 173 Plates, two of them splendidly Illuminated. Two
Volumes, small folio, half-morocco extra, £6 6s.; Large Paper copies, imperial
folio, half-morocco extra, £8 8s.

COTMAN'S ETCHINGS OF ARCHITECTURAL REMAINS,
chiefly Norman and Gothic, in various Counties in England, but principally in
Norfolk, with Descriptive Notices by DAWSON TURNER, and Architectural Observations by THOMAS RICKMAN. Two Vols., imperial folio, containing 240 spirited
Etchings, half-morocco, top edges gilt, £8 8s.

COTMAN'S LIBER STUDIORUM. A Series of Landscape
Studies and Original Compositions for the Use of Art Students, consisting of
40 Etchings, the greater part executed in "soft ground." Imperial folio, half-
morocco, £1 11s. 6d.; small paper copies, imperial 4to, half-morocco, 18s.

COWPER'S POETICAL WORKS. Including his Translation of
HOMER. Edited by the Rev. H. F. CARY. With Portrait and 18 Steel Engravings after HARVEY. Royal 8vo, cloth extra, gilt edges, 10s. 6d.

"I long to know your opinion of Cowper's Translation. The *Odyssey* especially
is surely very Homeric. What nobler than the appearance of Phœbus at the be-
ginning of the *Iliad*—lines ending with 'Dread sounding-bounding in the silver
bow'"?—CHARLES LAMB, *in a Letter to Coleridge.*

CRUIKSHANK "AT HOME." Tales and Sketches by the
most Popular Authors. With numerous Illustrations by GEORGE and ROBERT
CRUIKSHANK and ROBERT SEYMOUR. Also, CRUIKSHANK'S ODD VO-
LUME, or Book of Variety, Illustrated by Two Odd Fellows—SEYMOUR and
CRUIKSHANK. Four Vols. bound in Two, fcap. 8vo, cloth extra, gilt, 10s. 6d.

CRUIKSHANK'S COMIC ALMANACK. Complete in Two
SERIES: The FIRST from 1835 to 1843; the SECOND from 1844 to 1853. A Gathering of the BEST HUMOUR of THACKERAY, HOOD, MAYHEW, ALBERT SMITH,
A'BECKETT, ROBERT BROUGH, &c. With 2000 Woodcuts and Steel Engravings
by CRUIKSHANK, HINE, LANDELLS, &c. Crown 8vo, cloth gilt, two very thick
volumes, 15s.; or, separately, 7s. 6d. per volume.

CRUIKSHANK'S UNIVERSAL SONGSTER. The largest
Collection extant of the best Old English Songs (upwards of 5000). With 87
Engravings on Steel and Wood by GEORGE and R. CRUIKSHANK, and 8 Portraits.
Three Vols., 8vo, cloth extra, gilt, 21s.

CUSSANS' HANDBOOK OF HERALDRY. With Instructions for Tracing Pedigrees and Deciphering Ancient MSS.; Rules for the Appointment of Liveries, Chapters on Continental and American Heraldry, &c., &c. By JOHN E. CUSSANS. Illustrated with 360 Plates and Woodcuts. Crown 8vo, cloth extra, gilt and emblazoned, 7s. 6d.

CUSSANS' HISTORY OF HERTFORDSHIRE. A County History, got up in a very superior manner, and ranging with the finest works of its class. By JOHN E. CUSSANS. Illustrated with full-page Plates on Copper and Stone, and a profusion of small Woodcuts. Parts 1. to VI. are now ready, price 21s. each.

⁎ *An entirely new History of this important County, great attention being given to all matters pertaining to Family History.*

CUVIER'S ANIMAL KINGDOM, arranged after its Organization : forming a Natural History of Animals, and an Introduction to Comparative Anatomy. New Edition, with considerable Additions by W. B. CARPENTER and J. O. WESTWOOD. Illustrated by many Hundred Wood Engravings, and numerous Steel Engravings by THOS. LANDSEER, mostly Coloured. Imperial 8vo, cloth extra, 18s.

CYCLOPÆDIA OF COSTUME ; or, A Dictionary of Dress—Regal, Ecclesiastical, Civil, and Military—from the Earliest Period in England to the reign of George the Third. Including Notices of Contemporaneous Fashions on the Continent, and preceded by a General History of the Costumes of the Principal Countries of Europe. By J. R. PLANCHÉ, Somerset Herald. To be Completed in Twenty-four Parts, quarto, at Five Shillings each, profusely illustrated by Coloured and Plain Plates and Wood Engravings.—A full Prospectus will be sent upon application.

"This, the first number of a Cyclopædia of Ancient and Modern Costume, gives promise that the work, when complete, will be one of the most perfect works ever published upon the subject. The illustrations are numerous and excellent, and would, even without the letterpress, render the work an invaluable book of reference for information as to costumes for fancy balls and character quadrilles."—*Standard.*

"Destined, we anticipate, to be the standard English work on dress."—*Builder.*

"One of the most magnificent publications of its kind ever put before the public."—*Lloyd's News.*

"Promises to be a very complete work on a subject of the greatest importance to the historian and the archæologist."—*Tablet.*

"Beautifully printed and superbly illustrated."—*Standard*, second notice.

DICKENS' LIFE AND SPEECHES. Royal 16mo, cloth extra, 2s. 6d.

DICKENS' SPEECHES, Social and Literary, now first collected. Royal 16mo, cloth extra, 1s.

DISCOUNT TABLES, on a new and simple plan ; to facilitate the Discounting of Bills, and the Calculation of Interest on Banking and Current Accounts, &c. ; showing, without calculation, the number of days from every day in the year to any other day. By THOMAS READER. Post 8vo, cloth extra, 7s.

DODDRIDGE'S FAMILY EXPOSITOR ; or, A Paraphrase and Version of the New Testament, with Critical Notes. A New Edition, with Memoir of the Author by JOB ORTON and Dr. KIPPIS. Imperial 8vo, with Portrait, cloth extra, 12s.

DON QUIXOTE : A Revised Translation, based upon those of MOTTEUX, JARVIS, and SMOLLETT. With 50 Illustrations by ARMSTRONG and TONY JOHANNOT. Royal 8vo, cloth extra, gilt, 10s. 6d.

DON QUIXOTE IN SPANISH.—EL INGENIOSO HIDALGO DON QUIJOTE DE LA MANCHA. Nueva Edicion, corregida y revisada. Por MIGUEL DE CERVANTES SAAVEDRA. Complete in One Volume, post 8vo, nearly 700 pages, cloth extra, price 4s. 6d.

DRURY'S ILLUSTRATIONS of FOREIGN ENTOMOLOGY.
Containing, in 150 beautifully Coloured Plates, upwards of 600 Exotic Insects of the East and West Indies, China, New Holland, North and South America, Germany, &c. With important Additions and Scientific Indexes, by J. O. WEST-WOOD, F.L.S. Three Vols, 4to, half-morocco extra, £5 5s.

DULWICH GALLERY (The): A Series of 50 beautifully Coloured Plates, from the most celebrated Pictures in this Collection, executed by the Custodian, R. COCKBURN, and mounted upon Cardboard, in the manner of Drawings. Imperial folio, in portfolio, £16 16s.

DUNLOP'S HISTORY OF FICTION: Being a Critical and Analytical Account of the most celebrated Prose Works of Fiction, from the Earliest Greek Romances to the Novels of the Present Day, with General Index. Third Edition, royal 8vo, cloth extra, 9s.

EDGEWORTH'S **(Maria) TALES AND NOVELS,** Complete. Including "HELEN" (her last work). With 38 highly-finished Steel Engravings after HARVEY and others. Ten Vols., fcap. 8vo, cloth extra, gilt, £1 10s.
The volumes are sold separately at 3s. 6d. each, illustrated, as follows :—

Moral Tales.	Madame de Fleury, &c.
Popular Tales.	Patronage.
Belinda.	Comic Dramas, Leonora, &c.
Castle Rackrent, Irish Bulls, &c.	Harrington, Bores, &c.
Fashionable Life.	Helen.

"We do not know that Miss Edgeworth in the delineation of manners has, in the whole circle of literature, a rival, except the inimitable authors of Gil Blas and Don Quixote ; and the discrimination with which the individuality of her persons is preserved through all the varieties of rank, sex, and nation, gives to her stories a combined charm of truth and novelty, and creates an interest more acute than fiction (if fiction it can be called) ever excited."—*Quarterly Review.*

EDWARDS'S (Jonathan) COMPLETE WORKS. With an Essay on his Genius and Writings by HENRY ROGERS, and a Memoir by S. E. DWIGHT. Two Vols., imperial 8vo, with Portrait, cloth extra, £1 5s.

ELLIS'S (Mrs.) MOTHERS OF GREAT MEN. A New Edition, with Illustrations by VALENTINE BROMLEY. Crown 8vo, cloth gilt, 6s.

EMANUEL ON DIAMONDS AND PRECIOUS STONES ; Their History, Value, and Properties ; with Simple Tests for ascertaining their Reality. By HARRY EMANUEL, F.R.G.S. With numerous Illustrations, Tinted and Plain. A New Edition, crown 8vo, cloth extra, gilt, 6s.

ENGLISHMAN'S HOUSE (The): A Practical Guide to all interested in Selecting or Building a House, with full Estimates of Cost, Quantities, &c. By C. J. RICHARDSON. Third Edition. With nearly 600 Illustrations. Crown 8vo, cloth extra, 7s. 6d.
* *This book is intended to supply a long-felt want, viz., a plain, non-technical account of every style of house, with the cost and manner of building; it gives every variety, from a workman's cottage to a nobleman's palace.*

FARADAY'S **CHEMICAL HISTORY OF A CANDLE.** Lectures delivered to a Juvenile Audience. A New Edition, Edited by W. CROOKES, Esq., F.C.S., &c. Crown 8vo, cloth extra, with numerous Illustrations, 4s. 6d.

FARADAY'S VARIOUS FORCES OF NATURE. A New Edition, Edited by W. CROOKES, Esq., F.C.S., &c. Crown 8vo, cloth extra, with numerous Illustrations, 4s. 6d.

FIGUIER'S PRIMITIVE MAN : A Popular Manual of the prevailing Theories of the Descent of Man as promulgated by DARWIN, LYELL, Sir JOHN LUBBOCK, HUXLEY, E. B. TYLOR, and other eminent Ethnologists. Translated from the last French edition, and revised by E. B. T. With 263 Illustrations. Demy 8vo, cloth extra, gilt, 9s.

"An interesting and essentially popular résumé of all that has been written on the subject. M. Figuier has collected together the evidences which modern researches have accumulated, and has done this with a considerable amount of care."—*Athenæum.*

FINISH TO LIFE IN AND OUT OF LONDON ; or, The Final Adventures of Tom, Jerry, and Logic. By PIERCE EGAN. Royal 8vo, cloth extra, with spirited Coloured Illustrations by CRUIKSHANK, 21s.

FLAGELLATION AND THE FLAGELLANTS.—A History of the Rod in all Countries, from the Earliest Period to the Present Time. By the Rev. W. COOPER, B.A. Third Edition, revised and corrected, with numerous Illustrations. Thick crown 8vo, cloth extra, gilt, 12s. 6d.

FOOLS' PARADISE ; with the Many Wonderful Adventures there, as seen in the strange, surprising Peep-Show of Professor Wolley Cobble. Crown 4to, with nearly 350 very funny Coloured Pictures, cloth extra, gilt, 7s. 6d.

FOXE'S BOOK OF MARTYRS: The Acts and Monuments of the Church. Edited by JOHN CUMMING, D.D. With upwards of 1000 Illustrations. Three Vols., imperial 8vo, cloth extra, £2 12s. 6d.

FULLER'S (Rev. Andrew) COMPLETE WORKS. With Memoir by his Son. Imperial 8vo, with Portrait, cloth extra, 12s.

"He was a man whose sagacity enabled him to penetrate to the depths of every subject he explored ; whose conceptions were so powerful and luminous, that what was recondite and original appeared familiar ; what was intricate, easy and perspicuous,—in his hands ; equally successful in enforcing the practical, in stating the theoretical, and discussing the polemical branches of theology."—ROBERT HALL.

GELL'S TOPOGRAPHY OF ROME AND ITS VICINITY. A New Edition, revised and enlarged by E. H. BUNBURY. With a large mounted Map of Rome and its Environs (from a careful Trigonometrical Survey). Two Vols., 8vo, cloth extra, 15s.

"These volumes are so replete with what is valuable, that were we to employ our entire journal, we could, after all, afford but a meagre indication of their interest and worth. . . . . Learning, applied to the most patient personal research and actual examination of every foot of the interesting classic ground which the inquiry embraces, is the sure recommendation of this very able and standard work."—*Athenæum.*

GELL AND GANDY'S POMPEIANA ; or, The Topography, Edifices, and Ornaments of Pompeii. With upwards of 100 Line Engravings by GOODALL, COOKE, HEATH, PYE, &c. Demy 8vo, cloth extra, gilt, 18s.

GEMS OF ART : A Collection of 36 Engravings, after Paintings by REMBRANDT, CUYP, REYNOLDS, POUSSIN, MURILLO, TENIERS, CORREGGIO, GAINSBOROUGH, NORTHCOTE, &c., executed in Mezzotint by TURNER, BROMLEY, &c. Folio, in Portfolio, £1 11s. 6d.

GENIAL SHOWMAN ; or, Show Life in the New World. Adventures with Artemus Ward, and the Story of his Life. By E. P. HINGSTON. Third Edition. Crown 8vo, Illustrated by W. BRUNTON, cloth extra, 7s. 6d.

GIBBON'S ROMAN EMPIRE (The Decline and Fall of the). With Memoir of the Author, and full General Index. Imperial 8vo, with Portrait, cloth extra, 15s.

GILBERT'S (W. S.) DRAMATIC WORKS ("A Wicked World," &c., &c.). With numerous Illustrations by the Author. One Vol., crown 8vo, cloth extra. [*In preparation.*

GIL BLAS.—HISTORIA DE GIL BLAS DE SANTILLANA. Por Le Sage. Traducida al Castellano por el Padre Isla. Nueva Edicion, corregida y revisada. Complete in One Vol. Post 8vo, cl. extra, nearly 600 pp., 4s. 6d.

GILLRAY'S CARICATURES. Printed from the Original Plates, all engraved by Himself between 1779 and 1810; comprising the best Political and Humorous Satires of the Reign of George the Third, in upwards of 600 highly spirited Engravings. Atlas folio, half-morocco extra, gilt edges, £7 10s.—There is also a Volume of the Suppressed Plates, atlas folio, half-morocco, 31s. 6d.— Also, a Volume of Letterpress Descriptions, comprising a very amusing Political History of the Reign of George the Third, by Thos. Wright and R. H. Evans. Demy 8vo, cloth extra, 15s.; or half-morocco, £1 1s.

GILLRAY, THE CARICATURIST: The Story of his Life and Times, and Anecdotal Descriptions of his Engravings. Edited by Thomas Wright, Esq., M.A., F.S.A. With 83 full-page Plates, and numerous Wood Engravings. Demy 4to, 600 pages, cloth extra, 31s. 6d.

"High as the expectations excited by this description [in the Introduction] may be, they will not be disappointed. The most inquisitive or exacting reader will find ready gathered to his hand, without the trouble of reference, almost every scrap of narrative, anecdote, gossip, scandal, or epigram, in poetry or prose, that he can possibly require for the elucidation of the caricatures."—*Quarterly Review.*

GOLDEN LIBRARY.

Square 16mo (Tauchnitz size), cloth, extra gilt, price 2s. per vol.

CLERICAL ANECDOTES: The Humours and Eccentricities of "the Cloth."

HOLMES'S AUTOCRAT OF THE BREAKFAST TABLE. With an Introduction by George Augustus Sala.

HOLMES'S PROFESSOR AT THE BREAKFAST TABLE. With the Story of Iris.

HOOD'S WHIMS AND ODDITIES. Both Series Complete in One Volume, with all the original Illustrations.

LAMB'S ESSAYS OF ELIA. Both Series Complete in One Vol.

LEIGH HUNT'S ESSAYS: A Tale for a Chimney Corner, and other Pieces. With Portrait, and Introduction by Edmund Ollier.

SHELLEY'S COMPLETE WORKS, Prose and Poetical, reprinted from the Author's Original Editions, in Four Series: the First containing Queen Mab and the Early Poems, with Essay by Leigh Hunt; the Second containing Laon and Cythna, the Cenci, and Later Poems, with an Introductory Essay; the Third containing the Posthumous Poems, published by Mrs. Shelley in 1824; the Shelley Papers, published in 1833; The Wandering Jew, a Poem; the Notes to "Queen Mab," &c.; and the Fourth containing the Marlow and Dublin Pamphlets; the Six Weeks' Tour (1816); A Refutation of Deism, in a Dialogue (1814; and the two Novels, Zastrozzi and St. Irvyne, the last four now first included in any edition of Shelley. Price of each series, 2s.

GOLDEN TREASURY OF THOUGHT. An Encyclopædia of Quotations from Writers of all Times and all Countries. Selected and Edited by Theodore Taylor. Crown 8vo, cloth gilt, and gilt edges, 7s. 6d.

GOSPELS (The Holy). Illustrated with upwards of 200 Wood Engravings, after the best Masters, and every page surrounded by ornamental Borders. Handsomely printed, imperial 4to, cloth, full gilt (Grolier style), 15s.

GREENWOOD'S WILDS OF LONDON; Descriptive Sketches from Personal Observations and Experience of Remarkable Scenes, People, and Places in London. By James Greenwood, the "Lambeth Casual." With 12 Tinted Illustrations by Alfred Concanen. Crown 8vo, cloth extra, gilt, 7s. 6d.

"Mr. James Greenwood presents himself once more in the character of 'one whose delight it is to do his humble endeavour towards exposing and extirpating social abuses and those hole-and-corner evils which afflict society.'"—*Saturday Review.*

GREVILLE'S CRYPTOGAMIC FLORA. Comprising the Principal Species found in Great Britain, inclusive of all the New Species recently discovered in Scotland. Six Vols. royal 8vo, with 360 beautifully Coloured Plates, half-morocco, gilt, £7 7s. ; the Plates uncoloured, £4 14s. 6d.

" A truly admirable work, which may be honestly designated as so excellent, that nothing can be found to compete with it in the whole range of Indigenous Botany; whether we consider the importance of its critical discussions, the accuracy of the drawings, the minuteness of the analyses, or the unusual care which is evident in the publishing department."—LOUDON.

GRIMM.—GERMAN POPULAR STORIES. Collected by the Brothers GRIMM, and Translated by EDGAR TAYLOR. Edited, with an Introduction, by JOHN RUSKIN. With 22 Illustrations after the inimitable designs of GEO. CRUIKSHANK. Both Series Complete. Sq. cr. 8vo, 6s. 6d. ; gilt leaves, 7s. 6d.

" The illustrations of this volume . . . . are of quite sterling and admirable art, in a class precisely parallel in elevation to the character of the tales which they illustrate ; and the original etchings, as I have before said in the Appendix to my ' Elements of Drawing,' were unrivalled in masterfulness of touch since Rembrandt (in some qualities of delineation, unrivalled even by him). . . . . To make somewhat enlarged copies of them, looking at them through a magnifying glass, and never putting two lines where Cruikshank has put only one, would be an exercise in decision and severe drawing which would leave afterwards little to be learnt in schools."—*Extract from Introduction by* JOHN RUSKIN.

GULLIVER'S TRAVELS. By JONATHAN SWIFT. With Life of the Author, and numerous Wood Engravings. Demy 8vo, cloth extra, gilt, 5s.

GUYOT'S EARTH AND MAN ; or, Physical Geography in its Relation to the History of Mankind. With Additions by Professors AGASSIZ, PIERCE, and GRAY. With 12 Maps and Engravings on Steel, some Coloured, and copious Index. A New Edition. Crown 8vo, cloth extra, gilt, 4s. 6d.

HALL'S (Mrs. S. C.) SKETCHES OF IRISH CHARACTER. With numerous Illustrations on Steel and Wood, by DANIEL MACLISE, Sir JOHN GILBERT, W. HARVEY, and G. CRUIKSHANK. 8vo, cloth extra, gilt, 7s. 6d.

" The Irish sketches of this lady resemble Miss Mitford's beautiful English Sketches in ' Our Village,' but they are far more vigorous and picturesque and bright."—*Blackwood's Magazine.*

HARRIS'S AURELIAN ; A Natural History of English Moths and Butterflies, and the Plants on which they feed. A New Edition. Edited, with additions, by J. O. WESTWOOD. With about 400 exquisitely Coloured Figures of Moths, Butterflies, Caterpillars, &c., and the Plants on which they feed. Small folio, half-morocco extra, gilt edges, £3 13s. 6d.

HEEREN'S HISTORICAL WORKS. Translated from the German by GEORGE BANCROFT, and various Oxford Scholars. Six Vols., 8vo, cloth extra, £1 16s. ; or, separately, 6s. per volume.

** *The Contents of the Volumes are as follows:*—Vols. 1 and 2. Historical Researches into the Politics, Intercourse, and Trade of the Ancient Nations of Africa ; 3. Researches into the Politics, Intercourse, and Trade of the Ancient Nations of Africa, including the Carthaginians, Ethiopians, and Egyptians ; 4. History of the Political System of Europe and its Colonies ; 5. History of Ancient Greece, with Historical Treatises ; 6. A Manual of Ancient History, with special reference to the Constitutions, Commerce, and Colonies of the States of Antiquity.

" Prof. Heeren's Historical Researches stand in the very highest rank among those with which modern Germany has enriched European literature."—*Quarterly Review.*

" We look upon Heeren as having breathed a new life into the dry bones of Ancient History. In countries, the history of which has been too imperfectly known to afford lessons of political wisdom, he has taught us still more interesting lessons—on the social relations of men, and the intercourse of nations in the earlier ages of the world. His work is as learned as a professed commentary on the ancient historians and geographers, and as entertaining as a modern book of travels."—*Edinburgh Review.*

THE ORIGINAL HOGARTH.

HOGARTH'S WORKS. ENGRAVED BY HIMSELF. 153 fine Plates, with elaborate Letterpress Descriptions by JOHN NICHOLS. Atlas folio, half-morocco extra, gilt edges, £7 10s.

"I was pleased with the reply of a gentleman who, being asked which book he esteemed most in his library, answered 'Shakespeare;' being asked which he esteemed next best, answered 'Hogarth.'"—CHARLES LAMB.

HOGARTH'S WORKS. With Life and Anecdotal Descriptions of the Pictures, by JOHN IRELAND and JOHN NICHOLS. 160 Engravings, reduced in exact facsimile of the Originals. The whole in Three Series, 8vo, cloth, gilt, 22s. 6d.; or, separately, 7s. 6d. per volume.

HOGARTH MORALIZED : A Complete Edition of all the most capital and admired Works of WILLIAM HOGARTH, accompanied by concise and comprehensive Explanations of their Moral Tendency, by the late Rev. Dr. TRUSLER ; to which are added, an Introductory Essay, and many Original and Selected Notes, by JOHN MAJOR. With 57 Plates and numerous Woodcuts. New Edition, revised, corrected, and enlarged. Demy 8vo, hf.-Roxburghe, 12s. 6d.

HOGARTH'S FIVE DAYS' FROLIC ; or, Peregrinations by Land and Water. Illustrated by Tinted Drawings, made by HOGARTH and SCOTT during the Journey. Demy 4to, cloth extra, gilt, 10s. 6d.

HOGG'S JACOBITE RELICS OF SCOTLAND : Being the Songs, Airs, and Legends of the Adherents to the House of Stuart. Collected and Illustrated by JAMES HOGG. Two Vols., demy 8vo. The ORIGINAL EDITION. Cloth extra, 28s.

HOLBEIN'S PORTRAITS OF THE COURT OF HENRY THE EIGHTH. A Series of 80 exquisitely beautiful Tinted Plates, engraved by BARTOLOZZI, COOPER, and others, and printed on Tinted Paper, in imitation of the Original Drawings in the Royal Collection at Windsor. With Historical Letterpress by EDMUND LODGE, Norroy King of Arms. Imperial 4to, half-morocco extra, gilt edges, £5 15s. 6d.

HOLBEIN'S PORTRAITS OF THE COURT OF HENRY VIII. CHAMBERLAIN's Imitations of the Original Drawings, mostly engraved by BARTOLOZZI. 84 splendid Portraits, elaborately tinted in Colours, with Descriptive and Biographical Notes, by EDMUND LODGE, Norroy King of Arms. Atlas fol., half-morocco, gilt edges, £20.—The same, PROOF IMPRESSIONS, uncoloured, £18.

HONE'S SCRAP-BOOKS : The Miscellaneous Collections of WILLIAM HONE, Author of "The Table-Book," "Every-Day Book," and "Year-Book:" being a Supplementary Volume to those works. Now first published. With Notes, Portraits, and numerous Illustrations of curious and eccentric objects. Crown 8vo. [*In preparation.*

HOOD'S (Tom) FROM NOWHERE TO THE NORTH POLE : A Noah's Arkæological Narrative. By TOM HOOD. With 25 Illustrations by W. BRUNTON and E. C. BARNES. Square crown 8vo, in a handsome and specially-designed binding, gilt edges, 6s.

"Poor Tom Hood! It is very sad to turn over the droll pages of 'From Nowhere to the North Pole,' and to think that he will never make the young people, for whom, like his famous father, he ever had such a warm, sympathetic heart, laugh or cry any more. This is a birthday story, and no part of it is better than the first chapter, concerning birthdays in general, and Frank's birthday in particular. The amusing letterpress is profusely interspersed with the jingling rhymes which children love and learn so easily. Messrs. Brunton and Barnes do full justice to the writer's meaning, and a pleasanter result of the harmonious co-operation of author and artist could not be desired."—*Times.*

HOOKER'S (Sir William) EXOTIC FLORA. Containing Figures and Descriptions of Rare or otherwise interesting Exotic Plants. With Remarks upon their Generic and Specific Characters, Natural Orders, Culture, &c. Containing 232 large and beautifully Coloured Plates. Three Vols., imperial 8vo, cloth extra, gilt, £6 6s.

HOOKER AND GREVILLE'S. ICONES FILICUM; or,
Figures and Descriptions of Ferns, many of which have been altogether un-
noticed by Botanists, or have been incorrectly figured. With 240 beautifully
Coloured Plates. Two Vols., folio, half-morocco, gilt, £12 12s.

HOPE'S COSTUME OF THE ANCIENTS. Illustrated in
upwards of 320 Outline Engravings, containing Representations of Egyptian,
Greek, and Roman Habits and Dresses. A New Edition. Two Vols., royal 8vo,
cloth extra, £2 5s.

HORNE.—ORION. An Epic Poem, in Three Books. By RICHARD
HENGIST HORNE. With Photographic Portrait. TENTH EDITION. Crown 8vo,
cloth extra, 7s.

" Orion will be admitted, by every man of genius, to be one of the noblest, if not
the very noblest poetical work of the age. Its defects are trivial and conventional,
ts beauties intrinsic and supreme."—EDGAR ALLAN POE.

HOWE'S (Rev. John) COMPLETE WORKS. With Memoir of
his Life by Dr. CALAMY. Imperial 8vo, with Portrait, cloth extra, 15s.

HUGO'S (Victor) LES MISÉRABLES. Complete in Three
Parts.—Part I. FANTINE. Illustrated boards, 2s.—Part II. COSETTE
AND MARIUS. Illustrated boards, 2s.—Part III. ST. DENIS AND JEAN
VALJEAN. Illustrated boards, 2s. 6d.

" This work has something more than the beauties of an exquisite style or the
word-compelling power of a literary Zeus to recommend it to the tender care of a
distant posterity : in dealing with all the emotions, passions, doubts, fears, which go
to make up our common humanity, M. Victor Hugo has stamped upon every page
the Hall-mark of genius and the loving patience and conscientious labour of a true
artist. But the merits of ' Les Misérables ' do not merely consist in the conception
of it as a whole ; it abounds, page after page, with details of unequalled beauty."—
Quarterly Review.

HUGO'S (Victor) BY THE KING'S COMMAND. Complete
English Translation of " L'Homme qui Rit." Post 8vo, illustrated boards,
2s. 6d.   [*Nearly ready.*

HUME AND SMOLLETT'S HISTORY OF ENGLAND. With
a Memoir of HUME by himself, Chronological Table of Contents, and General
Index. Imperial 8vo, with Portraits of the Authors, cloth extra, 15s.

HUNT'S (Robert) DROLL STORIES OF OLD CORNWALL;
or, POPULAR ROMANCES OF THE WEST OF ENGLAND. With Illustrations by
GEORGE CRUIKSHANK. Crown 8vo, cloth extra, gilt, 7s. 6d.

ITALIAN SCHOOL OF DESIGN (The): 91 beautiful Plates,
chiefly Engraved by BARTOLOZZI, after Paintings in the Royal Collection by
MICHAEL ANGELO, DOMENICHINO, ANNIBALE CARACCI, and others. Imperial
4to, half-morocco, gilt edges, £2 12s. 6d.

JARDINE'S (Sir Wm.) NATURALIST'S LIBRARY. 42 vols.
fcap. 8vo, illustrated by over 1200 Coloured Plates, with numerous Portraits
and Memoirs of eminent Naturalists, half (imitation) calf, full gilt, top edges gilt,
£7 16s. ; or, separately, cloth extra, 4s. 6d. per vol., as follows :—

Vols. 1 to 4. British Birds; 5. Sun Birds: 6 and 7. Humming Birds ; 8. Game
Birds ; 9. Pigeons ; 10. Parrots : 11 and 12. Birds of West Africa ; 13. Fly
Catchers ; 14. Pheasants, Peacocks, &c. ; 15. Animals—Introduction ; 16. Lions
and Tigers ; 17. British Quadrupeds ; 18 and 19. Dogs ; 20. Horses ; 21 and 22.
Ruminating Animals ; 23. Elephants, &c. ; 24. Marsupialia ; 25. Seals, &c. ; 26.
Whales, &c. ; 27. Monkeys : 28. Insects—Introduction : 29. British Butterflies ;
30. British Moths, &c. : 31. Foreign Butterflies ; 32. Foreign Moths ; 33. Beetles ;
34. Bees ; 35. Fishes—Introduction, and Foreign Fishes ; 36 and 37. British
Fishes ; 38. Perch, &c. ; 39 and 40. Fishes of Guiana ; 41. Smith's Natural History
of Man : 42. Gould's Humming Birds.

JENNINGS' (Hargrave) ONE OF THE THIRTY. With numerous curious Illustrations. Crown 8vo, cloth extra, 10s. 6d.

JENNINGS' (Hargrave) THE ROSICRUCIANS: Their Rites and Mysteries. With Chapters on the Ancient Fire and Serpent Worshippers, and Explanations of Mystic Symbols in Monuments and Talismans of Primeval Philosophers. Crown 8vo, with 300 Illustrations, 10s. 6d.

JERROLD'S (Blanchard) CENT. PER CENT. A Story Written on a Bill Stamp. Fcap. 8vo, illustrated boards, 2s.

JERROLD'S (Douglas) THE BARBER'S CHAIR, AND THE HEDGEHOG LETTERS. Edited. with an Introduction, by his Son, BLANCHARD JERROLD. Crown 8vo, with Steel Plate Portrait, cloth extra, 7s. 6d.

"Better fitted than any other of his productions to give an idea of Douglas Jerrold's amazing wit : the 'Barber's Chair' may be presumed to give as near an approach as is possible in print to the wit of Jerrold's conversation."—*Examiner.*

"No library is complete without Douglas Jerrold's Works ; *ergo*, no library is complete without the 'Barber's Chair.' A delightful volume ; the papers are most amusing ; they abound with sly touches of sarcasm ; they are full of playful wit and fancy."—*Pictorial World.*

JERROLD'S (Douglas) BROWNRIGG PAPERS, AND MINOR STORIES. Edited by his Son, BLANCHARD JERROLD. Post 8vo, illustrated boards, 2s.

JOHNSON'S ENGLISH DICTIONARY. Printed verbatim from the Author's Last and most Complete Edition, with all the Examples in full ; to which are prefixed a History of the Language and a Grammar of the English Tongue. Imperial 8vo, cloth extra, 15s.

. *This is now the only complete edition of Johnson's Dictionary in print. For a critical view of the English Language it is indispensable.*

JOHNSON'S (Dr. Samuel) WORKS. With Life, by MURPHY. Two thick Vols., 8vo, with Portrait, cloth extra, 15s.

JOHNSON'S LIVES OF ENGLISH HIGHWAYMEN, PIRATES, AND ROBBERS. With Additions by WHITEHEAD. Fcap. 8vo, 16 Plates, cloth extra, gilt, 5s.

JOSEPHUS (The Works of). Translated by WHISTON. Containing both the "Antiquities of the Jews," and the "Wars of the Jews." Two Vols, 8vo, with 52 Illustrations and Maps, cloth extra, gilt, 14s.

KINGSLEY'S (Henry) New Novel, NUMBER SEVENTEEN. In Two Vols., crown 8vo, cloth extra, price 21s., will shortly be ready at all Libraries and at the Booksellers'.

KNIGHT'S (H. Gally) ECCLESIASTICAL ARCHITECTURE OF ITALY, from the time of Constantine to the Fifteenth Century, with Introduction and descriptive Text. Complete in Two Series ; the FIRST, to the end of the Eleventh Century ; the SECOND, from the Twelfth to the Fifteenth Century ; containing 81 beautiful Views of Ecclesiastical Buildings in Italy, several of them Illuminated in gold and colours. Imperial folio, half-morocco extra, price £3 13s. 6d. each Series.

"To the amateur of architecture, but especially to those who have visited, or may intend to visit Italy, this book will be found invaluable."—*Times.*

LAMB'S (Charles) COMPLETE WORKS, in Prose and Verse, reprinted from the Original Editions, with many pieces now first included in any Edition, and Notes and Introduction by R. H. SHEPHERD. With Two Portraits and facsimile of a page of the "Essay on Roast Pig." Crown 8vo, cloth extra, gilt, 7s. 6d.

"Is it not time for a new and final edition of Lamb's Works—a finer tribute to his memory than any monument in Edmonton churchyard? Lamb's writings, and more especially his fugitive productions, have scarcely yet escaped from a state of chaos."—*Westminster Review*, October, 1874.

"A complete edition of Lamb's writings, in prose and verse, has long been wanted, and is now supplied. The editor appears to have taken great pains to bring together Lamb's scattered contributions, and his collection contains a number of pieces which are now reproduced for the first time since their original appearance in various old periodicals."—*Saturday Review*.

"Reprinted with much care from the best editions, or collected from the various magazines and journals to which Elia was a welcome contributor, both prose and verse will be found delightful reading. The dramatic criticisms, in particular, are almost unrivalled in true taste and quaintly vigorous originality."—*Graphic*.

LAMB (Mary and Charles) : THEIR POEMS, LETTERS, and REMAINS. With Reminiscences and Notes by W. CAREW HAZLITT. With HANCOCK'S Portrait of the Essayist, Facsimiles of the Title-pages of the rare First Editions of Lamb's and Coleridge's Works, and numerous Illustrations. Crown 8vo, cloth extra, 10s. 6d.; Large Paper Copies, 21s.

"Must be consulted by all future biographers of the Lambs."—*Daily News*.

"Very many passages will delight those fond of literary trifles; hardly any portion will fail in interest for lovers of Charles Lamb and his sister."—*Standard*.

LANDSEER'S (Sir Edwin) ETCHINGS OF CARNIVOROUS ANIMALS. Comprising 38 subjects, chiefly Early Works, etched by his Brother THOMAS or his Father, with letterpress Descriptions. Royal 4to, cloth extra, 15s.

LEE (General Edward): HIS LIFE AND CAMPAIGNS. By his Nephew, EDWARD LEE CHILDE. With Steel-plate Portrait by JEENS, and elaborate Map. Post 8vo, 9s. [*Nearly ready*.

LEMPRIERE'S CLASSICAL DICTIONARY. Miniature Edition. Containing a Full Account of all Proper Names mentioned in Ancient Authors, and much Information respecting the Usages and Habits of the Greeks and Romans, corrected to the present state of knowledge. 18mo, embossed roan gilt, 5s.

LIFE IN LONDON; or, The Day and Night Scenes of Jerry Hawthorn and Corinthian Tom. WITH THE WHOLE OF CRUIKSHANK'S VERY DROLL ILLUSTRATIONS, in Colours, after the Originals. Crown 8vo, cloth extra, 7s. 6d.

LINTON (Mrs. E. Lynn) PATRICIA KEMBALL : A Novel. New and Popular Edition, with a Steel-plate Frontispiece. Crown 8vo, cloth extra, gilt, 6s.

"A very clever and well-constructed story, original and striking, and interesting all through. . . . A novel abounding in thought and power and interest."—*Times*.

"Perhaps the ablest novel published in London this year. . . . . . We know of nothing in the novels we have lately read equal to the scene in which Mr. Hamley proposes to Dora. . . . We advise our readers to send to the library for the story."—*Athenæum*.

"This novel is distinguished by qualities which entitle it to a place apart from the ordinary fiction of the day; . . . displays genuine humour, as well as keen social observation. . . . . Enough graphic portraiture and witty observation to furnish materials for half a dozen novels of the ordinary kind."—*Saturday Review*.

LINTON'S (Mrs.) JOSHUA DAVIDSON, CHRISTIAN AND COMMUNIST. Sixth Edition, with a New Preface. Small crown 8vo, cloth extra, 4s. 6d.

"In a short and vigorous preface, Mrs. Linton defends her notion of the logical outcome of Christianity as embodied in this attempt to conceive how Christ would have acted, with whom He would have fraternised, and who would have declined to receive Him, had He appeared in the present generation."—*Examiner.*

LITTLE LONDON DIRECTORY OF 1677. The Oldest Printed List of the Merchants and Bankers of London. Reprinted from the Rare Original, with an Introduction by John Camden Hotten. 16mo, binding after the original, 6s. 6d.

LONDON.—WILKINSON'S LONDINA ILLUSTRATA; or, Graphic and Historical Illustrations of the most Interesting and Curious Architectural Monuments of the City and Suburbs of London and Westminster (now mostly destroyed). Two Vols., imperial 4to, containing 207 Copperplate Engravings, with historical and descriptive Letterpress, half-bound morocco, top edges gilt, £5 5s.

*** *An enumeration of a few of the Plates will give some idea of the scope of the Work:*—St. Bartholomew's Church, Cloisters, and Priory, in 1393 ; St. Michael's, Cornhill, in 1421 ; St. Paul's Cathedral and Cross, in 1616 and 1656; St. John's of Jerusalem, Clerkenwell, 1660 ; Bunyan's Meeting House, in 1687 ; Guildhall, in 1517 ; Cheapside and its Cross, in 1547, 1585, and 1641 ; Cornhill, in 1599 ; Merchant Taylors' Hall, in 1599 ; Shakespeare's Globe Theatre, in 1612 and 1647 ; Alleyne's Bear Garden, in 1614 and 1647 ; Drury Lane, in 1792 and 1814 ; Covent Garden, in 1732, 1794, and 1809 ; Whitehall, in 1638 and 1697 ; York House, with Inigo Jones's Water Gate, circa 1626 ; Somerset House, previous to its alteration by Inigo Jones, circa 1600 : St. James's Palace, 1660 ; Montagu House (now the British Museum) before 1685, and in 1804.

LONGFELLOW'S PROSE WORKS, Complete. With Portrait and Illustrations by Valentine Bromley. 800 pages, crown 8vo, cloth gilt, 7s. 6d.

*** *This is by far the most complete edition ever issued in this country. "Outre-Mer" contains two additional chapters, restored from the first edition; while " The Poets and Poetry of Europe," and the little collection of Sketches entitled " Driftwood," are now first introduced to the English public.*

LOST BEAUTIES OF THE ENGLISH LANGUAGE. An Appeal to Authors, Poets, Clergymen, and Public Speakers. By Charles Mackay, LL.D. Crown 8vo, cloth extra, 6s. 6d.

LOTOS LEAVES: Original Stories, Essays, and Poems, by Wilkie Collins, Mark Twain, Whitelaw Reid, John Hay, Noah Brooks, John Brougham, P. V. Nasby, Isaac Bromley, and others. Profusely Illustrated by Alfred Fredericks, Arthur Lumley, John La Farge, Gilbert Burling, George White, and others. Crown 4to, handsomely bound, cloth extra, gilt and gilt edges, 21s.

"A very comely and pleasant volume, produced by general contribution of a literary club in New York, which has some kindly relations with a similar coterie in London. A *livre de luxe*, splendidly illustrated."—*Daily Telegraph.*

MACLISE'S GALLERY OF ILLUSTRIOUS LITERARY CHARACTERS. (The famous Fraser Portraits.) With Notes by the late William Maginn, LL.D. Edited, with copious additional Notes, by William Bates, B.A. The volume contains 83 Characteristic Portraits, now first issued in a complete form. Demy 4to, cloth gilt and gilt edges, 31s. 6d.

"One of the most interesting volumes of this year's literature."—*Times.*

"Deserves a place on every drawing-room table, and may not unfitly be removed from the drawing-room to the library."—*Spectator.*

MADRE NATURA versus THE MOLOCH OF FASHION.
By LUKE LIMNER. With 32 Illustrations by the Author. FOURTH EDITION, revised and enlarged. Crown 8vo, cloth, extra gilt, *2s. 6d.*

" Agreeably written and amusingly illustrated. Common sense and erudition are brought to bear on the subjects discussed in it."—*Lancet.*

MAGNA CHARTA. An exact Facsimile of the Original Document in the British Museum, printed on fine plate paper, nearly 3 feet long by 2 feet wide, with the Arms and Seals of the Barons emblazoned in Gold and Colours. Price *5s.*

A full Translation, with Notes, printed on a large sheet, price *6d.*

MANTELL'S PICTORIAL ATLAS OF FOSSIL REMAINS. With Additions and Descriptions. 4to, 74 Coloured Plates, cloth extra, *£1 11s. 6d.*

AUTHOR'S CORRECTED EDITION.

MARK TWAIN'S CHOICE WORKS. Revised and Corrected throughout by the Author. With Life, Portrait, and numerous Illustrations. 700 pages, cloth extra, gilt, *7s. 6d.*

MARK TWAIN'S PLEASURE TRIP on the CONTINENT of EUROPE. With Frontispiece. 500 pages, illustrated boards, *2s.*; or cloth extra, *2s. 6d.*

MARSTON'S (Dr. Westland) DRAMATIC and POETICAL WORKS. Collected Library Edition, in Two Vols., crown 8vo. [*In the Press.*

MARSTON'S (Philip Bourke) POEMS.

SONG TIDE, and other Poems. Second Edition. Crown 8vo, cloth extra, *8s.*

" This is a first work of extraordinary performance and of still more extraordinary promise. The youngest school of English poetry has received an important accession to its ranks in Philip Bourke Marston."—*Examiner.*

ALL IN ALL : Poems and Sonnets. Crown 8vo, cloth extra, *8s.*

" Many of these poems are leavened with the leaven of genuine poetical sentiment, and expressed with grace and beauty of language. A tender melancholy, as well as a penetrating pathos, gives character to much of their sentiment, and lends it an irresistible interest to all who can feel."—*Standard.*

MAXWELL'S LIFE OF THE DUKE OF WELLINGTON. Three Vols., 8vo, with numerous highly finished Line and Wood Engravings by Eminent Artists. Cloth extra, gilt, *£1 7s.*

MAYHEW'S LONDON CHARACTERS: Illustrations of the Humour, Pathos, and Peculiarities of London Life. By HENRY MAYHEW, Author of " London Labour and the London Poor," and other Writers. With nearly 100 graphic Illustrations by W. S. GILBERT and others. Crown 8vo, cloth extra, *6s.*

" Well fulfils the promise of its title. . . The book is an eminently interesting one, and will probably attract many readers."—*Court Circular.*

MEMORIALS OF MANCHESTER STREETS. By RICHARD WRIGHT PROCTER. With an Appendix, containing "The Cheetham Library," by JAMES CROSSLEY, F.S.A.; and " Old Manchester and its Worthies," by JAMES CROSTON, F.S.A. Demy 8vo, cloth extra, with Photographic Frontispiece and numerous Illustrations, *15s.*

MEYRICK'S ENGRAVED ILLUSTRATIONS OF ANCIENT ARMS AND ARMOUR. 154 highly finished Etchings of the Collection at Goodrich Court, Herefordshire, engraved by JOSEPH SKELTON, with Historical and Critical Disquisitions by Sir S. R. MEYRICK. Two Vols., imperial 4to, with Portrait, half-morocco extra, gilt edges, *£4 14s. 6d.*

MEYRICK'S PAINTED ILLUSTRATIONS OF ANCIENT

ARMS AND ARMOUR : A Critical Inquiry into Ancient Armour as it existed in Europe, but particularly in England, from the Norman Conquest to the Reign of Charles II. ; with a Glossary, by Sir S. R. MEYRICK. New and greatly improved Edition, corrected throughout by the Author, with the assistance of ALBERT WAY and others. Illustrated by more than 100 Plates, splendidly Illuminated in gold and silver ; also an additional Plate of the Tournament of Locks and Keys. Three Vols., imperial 4to, half-morocco extra, gilt edges, £10 10s.

"While the splendour of the decorations of this work is well calculated to excite curiosity, the novel character of its contents, the very curious extracts from the rare MSS. in which it abounds, and the pleasing manner in which the author's antiquarian researches are prosecuted, will tempt many who take up the book in idleness, to peruse it with care. No previous work can be compared, in point of extent, arrangement, science, or utility, with the one now in question. 1st. It for the first time supplies to our schools of art, correct and ascertained data for costume, in its noblest and most important branch—historical painting. 2nd. It affords a simple, clear, and most conclusive elucidation of a great number of passages in our great dramatic poets—ay, and in the works of those of Greece and Rome--against which commentators and scholiasts have been trying their wits for centuries. 3rd. It throws a flood of light upon the manners, usages, and sports of our ancestors, from the time of the Anglo-Saxons down to the reign of Charles the Second. And lastly, it at once removes a vast number of idle traditions and ingenious fables, which one compiler of history, copying from another, has succeeded in transmitting through the lapse of four or five hundred years.

" It is not often the fortune of a painful student of antiquity to conduct his readers through so splendid a succession of scenes and events as those to which Dr. Meyrick here successively introduces us. But he does it with all the ease and gracefulness of an accomplished *cicerone*. We see the haughty nobles and the impetuous knights — we are present at their arming—assist them to their shields—enter the well-appointed lists with them—and partake the hopes and fears, the perils, honours, and successes of the manly tournaments. Then we are presented to the glorious damsels, all superb and lovely, in ' velours and clothe of golde and dayntie devyces, bothe in pearls and emerawds, sawphires and dymondes,'— and the banquet, with the serving men and bucklers, servitors and trenchers—kings and queens—pageants, &c., &c. We feel as if the age of chivalry had returned in all its glory."—*Edinburgh Review.*

MILLINGEN'S ANCIENT INEDITED MONUMENTS;

comprising Painted Greek Vases, Statues, Busts, Bas-Reliefs, and other Remains of Grecian Art. 62 beautiful Engravings, mostly Coloured, with letterpress descriptions. Imperial 4to, half-morocco, £4 14s. 6d.

MILTON'S COMPLETE WORKS, Prose and Poetical. With an

Introductory Essay by ROBERT FLETCHER. Imperial 8vo, with Portraits, cloth extra, 15s.

" It is to be regretted that the prose writings of Milton should, in our time, be so little read. As compositions, they deserve the attention of every man who wishes to become acquainted with the full power of the English language. They abound with passages compared with which the finest declamations of Burke sink into insignificance. They are a perfect field of cloth of gold. The style is stiff with gorgeous embroidery. Not even in the earlier books of the ' Paradise Lost ' has the great poet ever risen higher than in those parts of his controversial works in which his feelings, excited by conflict, find a vent in bursts of devotional and lyric rapture. It is, to borrow his own majestic language, 'a sevenfold chorus of hallelujahs and harping symphonies.' "—MACAULAY.

MONTAGU'S (Lady Mary Wortley) LETTERS AND WORKS.

Edited by Lord WHARNCLIFFE. With important Additions and Corrections, derived from the Original Manuscripts, and a New Memoir. Two Vols., 8vo, with fine Steel Portraits, cloth extra, 18s.

" I have heard Dr. Johnson say that he never read but one book through from choice in his whole life, and that book was Lady Mary Wortley Montagu's Letters."—BOSWELL.

MONUMENTAL INSCRIPTIONS OF THE WEST INDIES, from the Earliest Date, with Genealogical and Historical Annotations, &c., from Original, Local, and other Sources. Illustrative of the Histories and Genealogies of the Seventeenth Century, the Calendars of State Papers, Peerages, and Baronetages. With Engravings of the Arms of the Principal Families. Chiefly collected on the spot by Capt. J. H. LAWRENCE-ARCHER. Demy 4to, cloth extra, 42s. [*Nearly ready.*]

MOSES' ANTIQUE VASES, Candelabra, Lamps, Tripods, Pateræ, Tazzas, Tombs, Mausoleums, Sepulchral Chambers, Cinerary Urns, Sarcophagi, Cippi, and other Ornaments. 170 Plates, several of which are coloured ; with historical and descriptive Letterpress by THOS. HOPE, F.A.S. Small 4to, cloth extra, 18s.

MUSES OF MAYFAIR : Vers de Société of the Nineteenth Century. Including Selections from TENNYSON, BROWNING, SWINBURNE, ROSSETTI, JEAN INGELOW, LOCKER, INGOLDSBY, HOOD, LYTTON, C.S.C., LANDOR, AUSTIN DOBSON, HENRY LEIGH, &c., &c. Edited by H. CHOLMONDELEY-PENNELL. Crown 8vo, cloth extra, gilt, gilt edges, 7s. 6d.

MYSTERY OF THE GOOD OLD CAUSE. Sarcastic Notices of those Members of the Long Parliament that held Places, both Civil and Military, contrary to the Self-denying Ordinance of April 3, 1645 ; with the Sums of Money and Lands they divided among themselves. Sm. 4to, half-morocco, 7s. 6d.

NAPOLEON III., THE MAN OF HIS TIME. From Caricatures. Part I. THE STORY OF THE LIFE OF NAPOLEON III., as told by J. M. HASWELL. Part II. THE SAME STORY, as told by the POPULAR CARICATURES of the past Thirty-five Years. Crown 8vo, with Coloured Frontispiece and over 100 Caricatures, 7s. 6d.

NATIONAL GALLERY (The). A Selection from its Pictures. By CLAUDE, REMBRANDT, CUYP, Sir DAVID WILKIE, CORREGGIO, GAINSBOROUGH, CANALETTI, VANDYCK, PAUL VERONESE, CARACCI, RUBENS, N. and G. POUSSIN, and other great Masters. Engraved by GEORGE DOO, JOHN BURNETT, WM. FINDEN, JOHN and HENRY LE KEUX, JOHN PYE, WALTER BROMLEY, and others. With descriptive Text. Columbier 4to, cl. extra, full gilt and gilt edges, 42s.

NEWTON'S (Rev. John) WORKS. With Life by the Rev. RICHARD CECIL, and Introduction by T. CUNNINGHAM. Imperial 8vo, with Portrait, cloth extra, 12s.

NICHOLSON'S FIVE ORDERS of ARCHITECTURE (The Student's Instructor for Drawing and Working the). Demy 8vo, with 41 Plates, cloth extra, 5s.

OLD BOOKS—FACSIMILE REPRINTS.

D'URFEY'S ("Tom") WIT AND MIRTH ; or, PILLS TO PURGE MELANCHOLY. Being a Collection of the best Merry Ballads and Songs, Old and New. Fitted to all Humours, having each their proper Tune for either Voice or Instrument ; most of the Songs being new set. London : Printed by W. Pearson, for J. Tonson, at Shakespeare's Head, over against Catherine Street in the Strand, 1719. An exact reprint. In Six Vols., large fcap. 8vo, printed on antique laid paper, antique boards, £3 3s.

EARLY NEWS SHEET.—The Russian Invasion of Poland in 1563. (Memorabilis et perinde stupenda de crudeli Moscovitarum Expeditione Narratio, e Germanico in Latinum conversa.) An exact facsimile of a contemporary account, with Introduction, Historical Notes, and full Translation. Large fcap. 8vo, antique paper, half-Roxburghe, 7s. 6d.

ENGLISH ROGUE (The), described in the Life of MERITON LATROON, and other Extravagants, comprehending the most Eminent Cheats of both Sexes. By RICHARD HEAD and FRANCIS KIRKMAN. A Facsimile Reprint of the rare Original Edition (1665-1672), with Frontispiece, Facsimiles of the 12 Copper-plates, and Portraits of the Authors. In Four Vols., large fcap. 8vo, printed on antique laid paper, and bound in antique boards, 36s.

OLD BOOKS—continued.

IRELAND FORGERIES.—Confessions of WILLIAM HENRY IRELAND. Containing the Particulars of his Fabrication of the Shakespeare Manuscripts: together with Anecdotes and Opinions (hitherto unpublished) of many Distinguished Persons in the Literary, Political, and Theatrical World. A Facsimile Reprint from the Original Edition, with several additional Facsimiles. Fcap. 8vo, printed on antique laid paper, and bound in antique boards, 10s. 6d.; a few Large Paper Copies, at 21s.

JOE MILLER'S JESTS: The politest Repartees, most elegant Bon-Mots, and most pleasing short Stories in the English Language. London: printed by T. Read. 1739. A Facsimile of the Original Edition. 8vo, half-morocco, 9s. 6d.

MUSARUM DELICIÆ; or, The Muses' Recreation, 1656; Wit Restored, 1658; and Wit's Recreations, 1640. The whole compared with the Originals. With all the Wood Engravings, Plates, Memoirs, and Notes. A New Edition, in Two Vols., large fcap. 8vo, printed on antique laid paper, and bound in antique boards, 21s.

RUMP (The) or, An Exact Collection of the Choicest POEMS and SONGS relating to the late Times, and continued by the most eminent Wits; from Anno 1639 to 1661. A Facsimile Reprint of the rare Original Edition (London, 1662), with Frontispiece and Engraved Title-page. In Two Vols., large fcap. 8vo, printed on antique laid paper, and bound in antique boards, 17s. 6d.

OLD DRAMATISTS.

BEN JONSON'S WORKS. With Notes, Critical and Explanatory, and a Biographical Memoir by WM. GIFFORD. Edited by Col. CUNNINGHAM. Complete in Three Vols., crown 8vo, cloth extra, gilt, with Portrait, 6s. each.

CHAPMAN'S (George) COMPLETE WORKS. Now first Collected. In Three Volumes, crown 8vo, cloth extra, with two Frontispieces, price 18s.; or, separately, 6s. per vol. Vol. I. contains the Plays complete, including the doubtful ones; Vol. II. the Poems and Minor Translations, with an Introductory Essay by ALGERNON CHARLES SWINBURNE; Vol. III. the Translations of the Iliad and Odyssey.

MARLOWE'S WORKS. Including his Translations. Edited, with Notes and Introduction, by Col. CUNNINGHAM. Crown 8vo, cloth extra, gilt, with Portrait, price 6s.

MASSINGER'S PLAYS. From the Text of WM. GIFFORD. With the addition of the Tragedy of "Believe as You List." Edited by Col. CUNNINGHAM. Crown 8vo, cloth extra, gilt, with Portrait, price 6s.

OLD SHEKARRY'S WORKS.

FOREST AND FIELD: Life and Adventure in Wild Africa. By the OLD SHEKARRY. With 8 Illustrations. Crown 8vo, cloth extra, gilt, 6s.

WRINKLES; or, Hints to Sportsmen and Travellers upon Dress, Equipment, Armament, and Camp Life. By the OLD SHEKARRY. A New Edition, with Illustrations. Small crown 8vo, cloth extra, gilt, 6s.

O**RIGINAL LISTS OF PERSONS OF QUALITY;** Emigrants; Religious Exiles; Political Rebels; Serving Men Sold for a Term of Years; Apprentices; Children Stolen; Maidens Pressed; and others who went from Great Britain to the American Plantations, 1600-1700. From MSS. in Her Majesty's Public Record Office. Edited by JOHN CAMDEN HOTTEN. Crown 4to, cloth gilt, 700 pages, 38s.; Large Paper Copies, half-morocco, 60s.

"This volume is an English Family Record, and as such may be commended to English families, and the descendants of English families, wherever they exist."—*Academy.*

O'SHAUGHNESSY'S (Arthur) POEMS.

AN EPIC OF WOMEN, and other Poems. Second Edition.
Fcap. 8vo, cloth extra, 6s.

LAYS OF FRANCE. (Founded on the "Lays of Marie.")
Second Edition. Crown 8vo, cloth extra, 10s. 6d.

MUSIC AND MOONLIGHT: Poems and Songs. Fcap. 8vo,
cloth extra, 7s. 6d.

" It is difficult to say which is more exquisite, the technical perfection of structure
and melody, or the delicate pathos of thought. Mr. O'Shaughnessy will enrich our
literature with some of the very best songs written in our generation."—*Academy.*

OTTLEY'S FACSIMILES OF SCARCE AND CURIOUS
PRINTS, by the Early Masters of the Italian, German, and Flemish Schools.
129 Copperplate Engravings, illustrative of the History of Engraving, from the
Invention of the Art (the Niellos printed in Silver). Imperial 4to, half-bound
morocco, top edges gilt, £6 6s.

OUIDA'S NOVELS.—Uniform Edition, crown 8vo, cloth extra,
gilt, price 5s. each.

Folle Farine.

Idalia. A Romance.

Chandos. A Novel.

Under Two Flags.

Cecil Castlemaine's Gage.

Tricotrin. The Story of a Waif
and Stray.

Pascarèl. Only a Story.

Held in Bondage ; or, Granville
de Vigne.

Puck. His Vicissitudes, Adventures, &c.

A Dog of Flanders, and other
Stories.

Strathmore ; or, Wrought by
his Own Hand.

Two Little Wooden Shoes.

PALEY'S COMPLETE WORKS. Containing the Natural
Theology, Moral and Political Philosophy, Evidences of Christianity, Horæ
Paulinæ, Clergyman's Companion, &c. Demy 8vo, with Portrait, cloth extra, 5s.

PARKS OF LONDON : their History, from the Earliest Period
to the Present Time. By JACOB LARWOOD. With numerous Illustrations,
Coloured and Plain. Crown 8vo, cloth extra, gilt, 7s. 6d.

PERCY'S RELIQUES OF ANCIENT ENGLISH POETRY.
Consisting of Old Heroic Ballads, Songs, and other Pieces of our Earlier Poets,
together with some few of later date, and a copious Glossary. Medium 8vo,
with Engraved Title and Frontispiece, cloth extra, gilt, 5s.

" The first time I could scrape a few shillings together I bought unto myself a
copy of these beloved volumes (*Percy's Reliques*) ; nor do I believe I ever read a
book half so frequently, or with half the enthusiasm."—Sir W. SCOTT.

PLAIN ENGLISH. By JOHN HOLLINGSHEAD, of the Gaiety
Theatre. Crown 8vo.   [*In preparation.*

PLATTNER'S MANUAL OF QUALITATIVE AND QUANTI-
TATIVE ANALYSIS WITH THE BLOWPIPE. From the last German
Edition. Revised and enlarged by Prof. TH. RICHTER, Royal Saxon Mining
Academy. Edited by T. HUGO COOKESLEY. With numerous Illustrations.
Demy 8vo, cloth extra, 21s.

PLUTARCH'S LIVES, Complete. Translated by the LANG-
HORNES. New Edition, with Medallion Portraits. In Two Vols., 8vo, cloth
extra, 10s. 6d.

POE'S (Edgar Allan) CHOICE PROSE AND POETICAL
WORKS. With BAUDELAIRE'S "Essay." 750 pages, crown 8vo, Portrait and
Illustrations, cloth extra, 7s. 6d.

PRACTICAL ASSAYER : A Guide to Miners and Explorers.
Giving directions, in the simplest form, for assaying bullion and the baser metals
by the cheapest, quickest, and best methods. By OLIVER NORTH. With Tables
and Illustrative Woodcuts. Crown 8vo, 7s. 6d.
"Likely to prove extremely useful. The instructions are clear and precise."—
Chemist and Druggist. "An admirable little volume."—*Mining Journal.*
"We cordially recommend this compact little volume to all engaged in mining
enterprise, and especially to explorers."—*Monetary and Mining Review.*

PRIVATE BOOK OF USEFUL ALLOYS AND MEMO-
RANDA FOR GOLDSMITHS AND JEWELLERS. By JAMES E. COLLINS,
C.E. Royal 16mo, 3s. 6d.

PROUT, FATHER.—THE FINAL RELIQUES OF FATHER
PROUT. Collected and edited, from MSS. supplied by the family of the Rev.
FRANCIS MAHONEY, by BLANCHARD JERROLD. Two Vols., cr. 8vo. [*In the Press.*

PUCK ON PEGASUS. By H. CHOLMONDELEY-PENNELL. Pro-
fusely illustrated by JOHN LEECH, H. K. BROWNE, Sir NOEL PATON, J. E.
MILLAIS, JOHN TENNIEL, RICHARD DOYLE, ELLEN EDWARDS, and other Artists.
Seventh Edition, crown 8vo, cloth extra, gilt, price 5s.
"The book is clever and amusing, vigorous and healthy."—*Saturday Review.*

PUGIN'S ARCHITECTURAL WORKS.

APOLOGY FOR THE REVIVAL OF CHRISTIAN ARCHI-
TECTURE. With 10 large Etchings. Small 4to, cloth extra, 5s.

EXAMPLES OF GOTHIC ARCHITECTURE, selected from
Ancient Edifices in England. 225 Engravings by LE KEUX, with descriptive
Letterpress by E. J. WILLSON. Three Vols., 4to, cloth extra, £3 13s. 6d.

FLORIATED ORNAMENTS. 31 Plates in Gold and Colours,
royal 4to, half-morocco, tooled back and sides, £1 16s.

GOTHIC ORNAMENTS. 90 Plates, by J. D. HARDING and
others. Royal 4to, half-bound, £1 16s.

ORNAMENTAL TIMBER GABLES. 30 Plates. Royal 4to,
cloth extra, 18s.

SPECIMENS OF GOTHIC ARCHITECTURE, from Ancient
Edifices in England. 114 Outline Plates by LE KEUX and others. With descriptive Letterpress and Glossary by E. J. WILLSON. Two Vols., 4to, cloth extra,
£1 16s.

TRUE PRINCIPLES OF POINTED OR CHRISTIAN
ARCHITECTURE. With 87 Illustrations. Small 4to, cloth extra, 10s. 6d.

PUNIANA. Edited by the Hon. HUGH ROWLEY. Contains
nearly 3000 of the best Riddles, and 10,000 most outrageous Puns. With numerous exquisitely fanciful Drawings. New Edition, small quarto, blue and
gold, gilt edges, 6s.

MORE PUNIANA ; or, Thoughts Wise and Other-Why's. A New
Collection of the best Riddles, Conundrums, Jokes, Sells, &c. Edited by the
Hon. HUGH ROWLEY. Containing upwards of Fifty beautifully executed Draw-
ings from his pencil. Small 4to, blue and gold, gilt edges, 6s.
"A witty, droll, and most amusing book, profusely and elegantly illustrated."—
Standard.

PURSUIVANT OF ARMS (The); or, Heraldry founded upon Facts. A Popular Guide to the Science of Heraldry. By J. R. PLANCHÉ, Esq., Somerset Herald. To which are added, Essays on the BADGES OF THE HOUSES OF LANCASTER AND YORK. With Coloured Frontispiece, five full-page Plates, and about 200 Illustrations. Crown 8vo, cloth extra, gilt, 7s. 6d.

QUEENS AND KINGS, AND OTHER THINGS: A Rare and Choice Collection of Pictures, Poetry, and strange but veritable Histories, designed and written by the Princess HESSE-SCHWARZBOURG. Imprinted in gold and many colours by the Brothers DALZIEL, at their Camden Press. Imperial 4to, cloth gilt and gilt edges, £1 1s.

RABELAIS' WORKS. Faithfully translated from the French, with variorum Notes, and numerous Characteristic Illustrations by GUSTAVE DORÉ. Crown 8vo, cloth extra, 700 pages, 7s. 6d.

READE'S (Winwood) THE OUTCAST. Cr. 8vo, cloth extra, 5s.

REMARKABLE TRIALS AND NOTORIOUS CHARACTERS. From "Half-Hanged Smith," 1700, to Oxford, who shot at the Queen, 1840. By Captain L. BENSON. With nearly Fifty spirited full-page Engravings by PHIZ. Crown 8vo, cloth extra, gilt, 7s. 6d.

ROCHEFOUCAULD'S REFLECTIONS & MORAL MAXIMS. With Introductory Essay by SAINTE-BEUVE, and Explanatory Notes. Royal 16mo, cloth extra, 1s. 6d.

ROLL OF BATTLE ABBEY; or, A List of the Principal Warriors who came over from Normandy with William the Conqueror, and Settled in this Country, A.D. 1066-7. Printed on fine plate paper, nearly three feet by two, with the principal Arms emblazoned in Gold and Colours. Price 5s.

ROLL OF CAERLAVEROCK, the Oldest Heraldic Roll; including the Original Anglo-Norman Poem, and an English Translation of the MS. in the British Museum. By THOMAS WRIGHT, M.A. The Arms emblazoned in Gold and Colours. In 4to, very handsomely printed, extra gold cloth, 12s.

ROMAN CATHOLICS IN THE COUNTY OF YORK IN 1604 (A LIST OF). Transcribed from the MS. in the Bodleian Library, and Edited, with Notes, by EDWARD PEACOCK, F.S.A. Small 4to, cloth extra, 15s.

ROSCOE'S LIFE AND PONTIFICATE OF LEO THE TENTH. Edited by his Son, THOMAS ROSCOE. Two Vols., 8vo, with Portraits and numerous Plates, cloth extra, 18s. [*New Edition preparing*.

ROSCOE'S LIFE OF LORENZO DE' MEDICI. called "THE MAGNIFICENT." A New and much improved Edition. Edited by his Son, THOMAS ROSCOE. Demy 8vo, with Portraits and numerous Plates, cloth extra, 9s.

ROSS'S (C. H.) STORY OF A HONEYMOON. With numerous Illustrations by the Author. Fcap. 8vo, illustrated boards, 2s.

SALA (George Augustus) ON COOKERY IN ITS HISTO-RICAL ASPECT. With very numerous Illustrations by the AUTHOR. Crown 4to, cloth extra, gilt. [*In preparation*.

SCHOLA ITALICA; or, Engravings of the finest Pictures in the Galleries at Rome. Imperial folio, with 40 beautiful Engravings after MICHAEL ANGELO, RAPHAEL, TITIAN, CARACCI, GUIDO, PARMIGIANO, &c., by VOLPATO and others, half-bound morocco extra, £2 12s. 6d.
⁎ *This is one of the most esteemed of the old collections of Italian line-engravings, and has hitherto been very scarce.*

SCHOOL LIFE AT WINCHESTER COLLEGE ; or, The Reminiscences of a Winchester Junior. By the Author of "The Log of the Water
Lily ;" and "The Water Lily on the Danube." Crown 8vo, cloth extra, gilt,
with full-page Coloured Illustrations, 7s. 6d.

**SCHOPENHAUER'S THE WORLD AS WILL AND IMA-
GINATION.** Translated by Dr. FRANZ HÜFFER, Author of "Richard Wagner
and the Music of the Future." [*In preparation.*

SCOTT'S COMMENTARY ON THE HOLY BIBLE. With
the Author's Last Corrections, and beautiful Illustrations and Maps. Three Vols.,
imperial 8vo, cloth extra, £1 16s.

"SECRET OUT" SERIES.

Crown 8vo, cloth extra, profusely Illustrated, price 4s. 6d. each.

ART OF AMUSING. A Collection of Graceful Arts, Games,
Tricks, Puzzles, and Charades. By FRANK BELLEW. 300 Illustrations.

HANKY-PANKY : Very Easy Tricks, Very Difficult Tricks, White
Magic, Sleight of Hand. Edited by W. H. CREMER. 200 Illustrations.

MAGICIAN'S OWN BOOK : Performances with Cups and Balls,
Eggs, Hats, Handkerchiefs, &c. All from Actual Experience. Edited by W. H.
CREMER. 200 Illustrations.

MAGIC NO MYSTERY: Tricks with Cards, Dice, Balls, &c.,
with fully descriptive working Directions. Numerous Illustrations.

MERRY CIRCLE (The) : A Book of New Intellectual Games and
Amusements. By CLARA BELLEW. Numerous Illustrations.

SECRET OUT : One Thousand Tricks with Cards, and other Recreations ; with entertaining Experiments in Drawing-room or "White Magic."
By W. H. CREMER. 300 Engravings.

SEYMOUR'S (Alfred) HUMOROUS SKETCHES. 86 Clever
and Amusing Caricature Etchings on Steel, with Letterpress Commentary by
ALFRED CROWQUILL. A New Edition, with Biographical Notice, and Descriptive List of Plates. Royal 8vo, cloth extra, gilt edges, 15s.

SHAKESPEARE, THE LANSDOWNE EDITION. Beauti-
fully printed in red and black, in small but very clear type. Post 8vo, with
engraved facsimile of DROESHOUT's Portrait, cloth extra, gilt, gilt edges, 14s.; or,
illustrated by 37 beautiful Steel Plates, after STOTHARD, cloth extra, gilt, gilt
edges, 18s.

SHAW'S ILLUMINATED WORKS.

**ALPHABETS, NUMERALS, AND DEVICES OF THE
MIDDLE AGES.** Selected from the finest existing Specimens. 4to, 48 Plates
(26 Coloured), £2 2s. : Large Paper, imperial 4to, the Coloured Plates very highly
finished and heightened with Gold, £4 4s. [*New Edition preparing.*

DECORATIVE ARTS OF THE MIDDLE AGES. Exhibiting,
in 41 Plates and numerous beautiful Woodcuts, choice Specimens of the various
kinds of Ancient Enamel, Metal Work, Wood Carvings, Paintings on Stained
Glass, Venetian Glass, Initial Illuminations, Embroidery, Fictile Ware, Book-
binding, &c. ; with elegant Initial Letters to the various Descriptions. Imperial
8vo, half-morocco extra, £1 8s.

DRESSES AND DECORATIONS OF THE MIDDLE AGES,
from the Seventh to the Seventeenth Centuries. 94 Plates, beautifully Coloured,
a profusion of Initial Letters, and Examples of Curious Ornament, with Historical
Introduction and Descriptive Text. Two Vols., imperial 8vo, half-Roxburghe,
£5 5s.

ENCYCLOPÆDIA OF ORNAMENT. Select Examples from the purest and best Specimens of all kinds and all Ages: 4to, 59 Plates, half-morocco, £1 1s.; Large Paper Copies, imperial 4to, with all the Plates Coloured, half-morocco, £2 12s. 6d.

ILLUMINATED ORNAMENTS OF THE MIDDLE AGES, from the Sixth to the Seventeenth Century. Selected from Missals, MSS., and early printed Books. 66 Plates, carefully coloured from the Originals, with Descriptions by Sir F. MADDEN, Keeper of MSS., Brit. Mus. 4to, half-Roxburghe, £3 13s. 6d.; Large Paper Copies, the Plates finished with opaque Colours and illuminated with Gold, imperial 4to, half-Roxburghe, £7 7s.

ILLUSTRATIONS OF DOMESTIC ARCHITECTURE IN ENGLAND, during the Reign of QUEEN ELIZABETH. Imperial 4to, 43 Plates of Architectural Ornament, and Portrait, half-morocco, £1 16s.; or India Proofs, half-morocco extra, £2 8s.

LUTON CHAPEL : A Series of 20 highly-finished Line Engravings of Gothic Architecture and Ornaments. Imperial folio, India Proofs, half-morocco, £2 8s.

ORNAMENTAL TILE PAVEMENTS, drawn from existing authorities. Imperial 4to, 47 large Coloured Plates, half-morocco, £1 16s.

SPECIMENS OF ANCIENT FURNITURE, drawn from existing authorities. With Descriptions by Sir S. R. MEYRICK. 4to, 74 Plates, half-morocco, £1 11s. 6d.; or, with some Plates Coloured, 4to, half-morocco, £2 2s.; Large Paper Copies, imperial 4to, all the Plates extra finished in opaque Colours, half-morocco extra, £4 14s. 6d.

SPECIMENS OF THE DETAILS OF ELIZABETHAN ARCHITECTURE. With Descriptive Letterpress by T. MOULE. 4to, 60 Plates, half-morocco, £1 5s.; Large Paper, imperial 4to, several of the Plates Coloured, half-morocco, £2 12s. 6d.

SHAW AND BRIDGENS' DESIGNS FOR FURNITURE, with Candelabra and Interior Decoration. 60 Plates, royal 4to, half-morocco, £1 1s.; Large Paper, imperial 4to, the Plates Coloured, half-morocco, £2 8s.

SHELLEY'S EARLY LIFE. From Original Sources. With Curious Incidents, Letters, and Writings, now First Collected. By D. F. MACCARTHY. Crown 8vo, with Illustrations, cloth extra, 7s. 6d.,

SHERIDAN'S COMPLETE WORKS, with Life and Anecdotes. Including his Dramatic Writings, printed from the Original Editions, his Works in Prose and Poetry, Translations, Speeches, Jokes, Puns, &c.; with a Collection of Sheridaniana. Crown 8vo, cloth extra, gilt, with 10 full-page tinted Illustrations, 7s. 6d.

"Whatever Sheridan has done, has been, *par excellence*, always the *best* of its kind. He has written the best comedy (School for Scandal), the *best* drama (the Duenna), the *best* farce (the Critic), and the *best* address (Monologue on Garrick); and, to crown all, delivered the very best oration (the famous Begum Speech) ever conceived or heard in this country."—BYRON.

"The editor has brought together within a manageable compass not only the seven plays by which Sheridan is best known, but a collection also of his poetical pieces which are less familiar to the public, sketches of unfinished dramas, selections from his reported witticisms, and extracts from his principal speeches. To these is prefixed a short but well-written memoir, giving the chief facts in Sheridan's literary and political career; so that with this volume in his hand, the student may consider himself tolerably well furnished with all that is necessary for a general comprehension of the subject of it."—*Pall Mall Gazette.*

SIGNBOARDS: Their History. With Anecdotes of Famous Taverns and Remarkable Characters. By JACOB LARWOOD and JOHN CAMDEN HOTTEN. With nearly 100 Illustrations. SEVENTH EDITION. Crown 8vo, cloth extra, 7s. 6d.

"Even if we were ever so maliciously inclined, we could not pick out all Messrs. Larwood and Hotten's plums, because the good things are so numerous as to defy the most wholesale depredation."—*The Times.*

SILVESTRE'S UNIVERSAL PALEOGRAPHY; or, A Collection of Facsimiles of the Writings of every Age. Containing upwards of 300 large and beautifully executed Facsimiles, taken from Missals and other MSS., richly Illuminated in the finest style of art. A New Edition, arranged under the direction of Sir F. MADDEN, Keeper of MSS., Brit. Mus. Two Vols., atlas folio, half-morocco, gilt, £31 10s.—Also, a Volume of HISTORICAL AND DESCRIPTIVE LETTERPRESS, by CHAMPOLLION FIGEAC and CHAMPOLLION, Jun. Translated, with additions, by Sir F. MADDEN. Two Vols., royal 8vo, half-morocco, gilt, £2 8s.

*** *This is one of the grandest books in the world, and cost nearly twenty thousand pounds in getting up. The finest possible specimens are given of MSS. in every European and Oriental language. The number of reproductions of French, German, and Italian miniatures is very considerable, while of such languages as Greek and Latin many specimens of every century and every style are given.*

SLANG DICTIONARY (The): Etymological, Historical, and Anecdotal. An ENTIRELY NEW EDITION, revised throughout, and considerably Enlarged. Crown 8vo, cloth extra, gilt, 6s. 6d.

"We are glad to see the Slang Dictionary reprinted and enlarged. From a high scientific point of view this book is not to be despised. Of course it cannot fail to be amusing also. It contains the very vocabulary of unrestrained humour, and oddity, and grotesqueness. In a word, it provides valuable material both for the student of language and the student of human nature."—*Academy.*

"In every way a great improvement on the edition of 1864. Its uses as a dictionary of the very vulgar tongue do not require to be explained."—*Notes and Queries.*

"Compiled with most exacting care, and based on the best authorities."—*Standard.*

SMITH'S HISTORICAL AND LITERARY CURIOSITIES: Containing Facsimiles of Autographs, Scenes of Remarkable Events, Interesting Localities, Old Houses, Portraits, Illuminated and Missal Ornaments, Antiquities, &c. 4to, with 100 Plates (some Illuminated), half-morocco extra, £2 5s.

*** *The Autographs are chiefly of a literary character, and include Letters by Coverdale, Sir Christopher Wren, Sir Isaac Newton, Cowley, Pope, Addison, Gray, Milton, Prior, Smollett, Sterne, Locke, Burns, Steele, Hume, Dr. Johnson, Benjamin Franklin, William Penn, &c.*

SMITH (Thomas Assheton), REMINISCENCES of the LATE; or, The Pursuits of an English Country Gentleman. By Sir J. E. EARDLEY WILMOT, Bart. New Edition, with Portrait, and plain and coloured Illustrations. Crown 8vo, cloth extra, 7s. 6d.

SMOKER'S TEXT-BOOK. By J. HAMER, F.R.S.L. Exquisitely printed from "silver-faced" type, cloth, very neat, gilt edges, 2s. 6d.

SOUTH'S (Dr. Robert) SERMONS. With Biographical Memoir, Analytical Tables, General Index, &c. Two Vols., royal 8vo, cloth extra, 15s.

SOUTHEY'S COMMON-PLACE BOOK. Edited by his Son-in-Law, J. W. WARTER. Second Edition. Four Vols., medium 8vo, with Portrait, cloth extra, £1 10s.

SOWERBY'S MANUAL OF CONCHOLOGY: A Complete Introduction to the Science. Illustrated by upwards of 650 etched Figures of Shells and numerous Woodcuts. With copious Explanations, Tables, Glossary, &c. 8vo, cloth extra, gilt, 15s. ; or, the Plates beautifully Coloured, £1 8s.

⁎⁎ This is the only work which, in a moderate compass, gives a comprehensive view of Conchology, according to the present advanced state of the science. It will not only be found useful to all who wish to acquire an elementary acquaintance with the subject, but also to the proficient, as a book of reference.

SPECTATOR (The), with the Original Dedications, Notes, and a General Index. Demy 8vo, with Portrait of Addison, cloth extra, 9s.

STEPHENS' BRITISH ENTOMOLOGY; or, A Synopsis of British Insects. Arranged in two great Classes of Haustellata and Mandibulata. Containing their Generic and Specific Distinctions: with an Account of their Metamorphoses, Times of Appearance, Localities, Food and Economy. Twelve Vols., 8vo, with 100 beautifully Coloured Plates, half-morocco, £8 8s.

⁎⁎ This work gives, in a systematic form, descriptions, both generic and specific, of all the Insects which have hitherto been found in Great Britain and Ireland : to these descriptions are appended coloured figures of some of the rarer and more interesting species, as well as localities and general notices of their food and economy, metamorphoses, periods of flight, appearance, &c.

"Mr. Stephens' work is of very high character, we might justly say the highest. We cannot, therefore, too strongly recommend it."—*Athenæum.*

STOTHARD'S MONUMENTAL EFFIGIES OF GREAT BRITAIN, selected from our Cathedrals and Churches. With Historical Description and Introduction, by John Kempe, F.S.A. A New Edition, with a large body of Additional Notes by John Hewitt. Imperial 4to, containing 147 beautifully finished Etchings, all tinted, and some Illuminated in Gold and Colours, half-morocco, £9 9s. ; Large Paper, half-morocco, £15 15s. [*In preparation.*

"No English library should be without this unique and important publication. Charles Stothard is the model which every antiquarian artist must follow, if he wishes to excel. His pencil was always guided by his mind, and we may safely assert that no one ever united equal accuracy and feeling."—*Quarterly Review.*

"It is only in the beautiful work on Monumental Effigies, by Stothard, that everything has been done which fidelity and taste could effect."—Shaw.

STRUTT'S DRESSES AND HABITS OF THE ENGLISH, from the Establishment of the Saxons in Britain to the Present Time. With an Historical Inquiry into every branch of Costume, Ancient and Modern. New Edition, with Explanatory Notes by J. R. Planché, Somerset Herald. Two Vols., royal 4to, with 153 Engravings from the most Authentic Sources, beautifully Coloured, half-Roxburghe, £6 6s. ; or the Plates splendidly Illuminated in Silver and Opaque Colours, in the Missal style, half-Roxburghe, £15 15s.

STRUTT'S REGAL AND ECCLESIASTICAL ANTIQUITIES OF ENGLAND : Authentic Representations of all the English Monarchs, from Edward the Confessor to Henry the Eighth ; with many Great Personages eminent under their several Reigns. New Edition, with critical Notes by J. R. Planché, Somerset Herald. Royal 4to, with 72 Engravings from Manuscripts, Monuments, &c., beautifully Coloured, half-Roxburghe, £3 3s. ; or the Plates splendidly Illuminated in Gold and Colours, half-morocco, £10 10s.

STUBBS' ANATOMY OF THE HORSE. 24 fine Copper-plate Engravings on a very large scale. Imperial folio, cloth extra, £1 1s.

SUMMER CRUISING IN THE SOUTH SEAS. By Charles Warren Stoddard. With Twenty-five Illustrations by Wallis Mackay. Crown 8vo, cloth, extra gilt, 7s. 6d.

"This is a very amusing book, and full of that quiet humour for which the Americans are so famous. We have not space to enumerate all the picturesque descriptions, the poetical thoughts, which have so charmed us in this volume ; but we recommend our readers to go to the South Seas with Mr. Stoddard in his prettily illustrated and amusingly written little book."—*Vanity Fair.*

SYNTAX'S (Dr.) THREE TOURS, in Search of the Picturesque, in Search of Consolation, and in Search of a Wife. With the whole of ROWLANDSON'S droll full-page Illustrations, in Colours, and Life of the Author by J. C. HOTTEN. Medium 8vo, cloth extra, gilt, 7s. 6d.

SWINBURNE'S WORKS.

BOTHWELL: A Tragedy. By ALGERNON CHARLES SWINBURNE. SECOND EDITION. Crown 8vo, cloth extra, 12s. 6d.

"Mr. Swinburne's most prejudiced critic cannot, we think, deny that 'Bothwell' is a poem of a very high character. Every line bears traces of power, individuality, and vivid imagination. The versification, while characteristically supple and melodious, also attains, in spite of some affectations, to a sustained strength and dignity of a remarkable kind. Mr. Swinburne is not only a master of the music of language, but he has that indescribable touch which discloses the true poet—the touch that lifts from off the ground."—*Saturday Review.*

ESSAYS AND STUDIES. Crown 8vo, 10s. 6d. [*In the press.*

GEORGE CHAPMAN: An Essay. Crown 8vo, 7s.

SONGS OF TWO NATIONS: A SONG OF ITALY, ODE ON THE FRENCH REPUBLIC, DIRÆ. Crown 8vo, 6s.

CHASTELARD: A Tragedy. Fcap. 8vo, 7s.

POEMS AND BALLADS. Fcap. 8vo, 9s.

NOTES ON "POEMS AND BALLADS," and on the Reviews of Them. Demy 8vo, 1s.

SONGS BEFORE SUNRISE. Crown 8vo, 10s. 6d.

ATALANTA IN CALYDON. A New Edition. Crown 8vo, 6s.

THE QUEEN MOTHER AND ROSAMOND. Fcap. 8vo, 5s.

UNDER THE MICROSCOPE. Post 8vo, 2s. 6d.

WILLIAM BLAKE: A Critical Essay. With Facsimile Paintings, Coloured by Hand, after Drawings by BLAKE and his Wife. Demy 8vo, 16s.

TAYLOR'S HISTORY OF PLAYING CARDS: Ancient and Modern Games, Conjuring, Fortune-Telling, and Card Sharping, Gambling and Calculation, Cartomancy, Old Gaming-Houses, Card Revels and Blind Hookey, Picquet and Vingt-et-un, Whist and Cribbage, Tricks, &c. With Sixty curious Illustrations. Crown 8vo, cloth extra, gilt, price 7s. 6d.

TAYLOR'S (Jeremy) COMPLETE WORKS. With Biographical and Critical Essay. Three Vols., imperial 8vo, with Portrait, cloth extra, £2 5s.

THACKERAYANA: Notes and Anecdotes. Illustrated by a profusion of Sketches by WILLIAM MAKEPEACE THACKERAY, depicting Humorous Incidents in his School-life, and Favourite Characters in the books of his every-day reading. Large post 8vo, with Hundreds of Wood Engravings, NOW FIRST PUBLISHED, from Mr. Thackeray's Original Drawings, cloth, full gilt, gilt top, 12s. 6d.

"An exceedingly curious and valuable volume, the diverting pages of which are adorned by some six hundred engraved facsimiles of the little caricature sketches which the illustrious author of 'Vanity Fair' was perpetually scribbling in the margins of books, and on every scrap of paper which came in his way, and which these eyes have witnessed him scribbling scores of times."—"*Echoes of the Week*," *in the Illustrated London News.*

THEODORE HOOK'S CHOICE HUMOROUS WORKS, with his Ludicrous Adventures, Bons-mots, Puns, and Hoaxes. With a new Life of the Author, Portraits, Facsimiles, and Illustrations. Cr. 8vo, cloth extra, gilt, 7s. 6d.

"As a wit and humourist of the highest order his name will be preserved. His political songs and *jeux d'esprit will form a volume of sterling and lasting attraction!*"—J. G. LOCKHART.

THESEUS : A GREEK FAIRY LEGEND. Illustrated, in a series of Designs in Gold and Sepia, by JOHN MOYR SMITH. With Descriptive Text. Oblong folio, price 7s. 6d.

THIERS' HISTORY OF THE CONSULATE AND EMPIRE OF FRANCE UNDER NAPOLEON. Roy. 8vo, cloth extra, 15s.

THIERS' HISTORY OF THE FRENCH REVOLUTION. Roy. 8vo, cloth extra, 15s.

"The History of the French Revolution by Thiers is a celebrated and popular book in France—and I believe in Europe. His was, in the highest degree, one of that quality of minds which take a marvellous grasp of all things—rapid in the acquirement of knowledge—one of those fine and unsullied pages on which so much may be written. He set himself to examine into the facts and the men of the Revolution. He inquired into its laws, its orations, its battles, its victories, its defeats. War he discussed with the generals—finances with the financiers – diplomacy with the diplomatists. Nothing escaped his enthusiastic, persevering, and enlightened mind. It combines the compactness and unity of the book, the order and arrangement of the journal, the simplicity of the biography, the valuable and minute details of the autobiography, and the enthusiasm, the passion, and the indignation of the pamphlet. There are in many parts of this great book, whole chapters which read as if they had been written with the sword."—JULES JANIN, *in the Athenæum.*

THORNBURY.—ON THE SLOPES OF PARNASSUS. By WALTER THORNBURY. Illustrated by J. E. MILLAIS, F. SANDYS, FRED. WALKER, G. J. PINWELL, J. D. HOUGHTON, E. J. POYNTER, H. S. MARKS, J. WHISTLER, and others. Handsomely printed, crown 4to, cloth extra, gilt and gilt edges, 21s. [*In preparation.*

TIMBS' ENGLISH ECCENTRICS and ECCENTRICITIES : Stories of Wealth and Fashion, Delusions, Impostures and Fanatic Missions, Strange Sights and Sporting Scenes, Eccentric Artists, Theatrical Folks, Men of Letters, &c. By JOHN TIMBS, F.S.A. With nearly 50 Illustrations. Crown 8vo, cloth extra, 7s. 6d.

"The reader who would fain enjoy a harmless laugh in some very odd company might do much worse than take an occasional dip into 'English Eccentrics.' Beaux, preachers, authors, actors, monstrosities of the public shows, and leaders of religious impostures, will meet him here in infinite, almost perplexing, variety. The queer illustrations, from portraits and caricatures of the time, are admirably suited to the letterpress."—*Graphic.*

TIMBS' CLUBS AND CLUB LIFE IN LONDON. With ANECDOTES of its FAMOUS COFFEE HOUSES, HOSTELRIES, and TAVERNS. By JOHN TIMBS, F.S.A. With numerous Illustrations. Crown 8vo, cloth extra, 7s. 6d.

TOURNEUR'S (Cyril) COLLECTED WORKS, including a hitherto altogether unknown Poem. Edited by J. CHURTON COLLINS. Post 8vo, antique boards. [*In preparation.*

TURNER'S (J. M. W.) LIBER FLUVIORUM; or, River Scenery of France. 62 highly-finished Line Engravings by WILLMORE, GOODALL, MILLER, COUSENS, and other distinguished Artists. With descriptive Letterpress by LEITCH RITCHIE, and Memoir by ALARIC A. WATTS. Imperial 8vo, cloth extra, gilt edges, £1 11s. 6d.

TURNER (J. M. W.) and GIRTIN'S RIVER SCENERY. 20 beautiful Mezzotinto Plates, engraved on Steel by REYNOLDS, BROMLEY, LUPTON, and CHARLES TURNER, principally after the Drawings of J. M. W. TURNER. Small folio, in Portfolio, £1 11s. 6d.

TURNER'S (J. M. W.) LIFE AND CORRESPONDENCE. Founded upon Letters and Papers furnished by his Friends and Fellow-Academicians. By WALTER THORNBURY. New Edition, entirely rewritten and added to. With numerous Illustrations. Two Vols., 8vo, cloth extra. [*In preparation.*

TURNER GALLERY (The) : A Series of Sixty Engravings from the Principal Works of JOSEPH MALLORD WILLIAM TURNER. With a Memoir and Illustrative Text by RALPH NICHOLSON WORNUM, Keeper and Secretary, National Gallery. Handsomely half-bound, India Proofs, royal folio, £10 ; Large Paper copies, Artists' India Proofs, elephant folio, £20.—A Descriptive Pamphlet will be sent upon application.

VAGABONDIANA ; or, Anecdotes of Mendicant Wanderers through the Streets of London ; with Portraits of the most Remarkable, drawn from the Life by JOHN THOMAS SMITH, late Keeper of the Prints in the British Museum. With Introduction by FRANCIS DOUCE, and Descriptive Text. With the Woodcuts and the 32 Plates, from the original Coppers. Crown 4to, half-Roxburghe, 12s. 6d.

VYNER'S NOTITIA VENATICA : A Treatise on Fox-Hunting, the General Management of Hounds, and the Diseases of Dogs ; Distemper and Rabies ; Kennel Lameness, &c. By ROBERT C. VYNER. Sixth Edition, Enlarged. With spirited Coloured Illustrations by ALKEN. Royal 8vo, cloth extra, 21s.

WALPOLE'S (Horace) ANECDOTES OF PAINTING IN ENGLAND. With some Account of the principal English Artists, and incidental Notices of Sculptors, Carvers, Enamellers, Architects, Medallists, Engravers, &c. With Additions by the Rev. JAMES DALLAWAY. New Edition, Revised and Edited, with Additional Notes, by RALPH N. WORNUM, Keeper and Secretary, National Gallery. Three Vols., 8vo, with upwards of 150 Portraits and Plates, cloth extra, £1 7s.

WALPOLE'S (Horace) ENTIRE CORRESPONDENCE. Chronologically arranged, with the Prefaces and Notes of CROKER, Lord DOVER, and others ; the Notes of all previous Editors, and Additional Notes by PETER CUNNINGHAM. Nine Vols., 8vo, with numerous fine Portraits engraved on Steel, cloth extra, £4 1s.

"The charm which lurks in Horace Walpole's Letters is one for which we have no term ; and our Gallic neighbours seem to have engrossed both the word and the quality—'elles sont piquantes' to the highest degree. If you read but a sentence, you feel yourself spell-bound till you have read the volume."—*Quarterly Review.*

WALTON AND COTTON, ILLUSTRATED.—THE COM-PLETE ANGLER ; or, The Contemplative Man's Recreation : Being a Discourse of Rivers, Fish-ponds, Fish and Fishing, written by IZAAK WALTON ; and Instructions how to Angle for a Trout or Grayling in a clear Stream, by CHARLES COTTON. With Original Memoirs and Notes by Sir HARRIS NICOLAS, K.C.M.G. With the 61 Plate Illustrations, precisely as in Pickering's two-volume Edition. Complete in One Volume, large crown 8vo, cloth antique, 7s. 6d.

WALT WHITMAN'S LEAVES OF GRASS. Complete in One thick Volume, 8vo, green cloth, 9s.

WARRANT TO EXECUTE CHARLES I. An exact Facsimile of this important Document, with the Fifty-nine Signatures of the Regicides, and corresponding Seals, on paper to imitate the Original, 22 in. by 14 in. Price 2s.

WARRANT TO EXECUTE MARY QUEEN OF SCOTS. An Exact Facsimile of this important Document, including the Signature of Queen Elizabeth and Facsimile of the Great Seal, on tinted paper, to imitate the Original MS. Price 2s.

WATERFORD ROLL (The).—Illuminated Charter-Roll of Waterford, Temp. Richard II. The Illuminations accurately Traced and Coloured for the Work from a Copy carefully made by the late GEORGE V. DU NOYER, Esq., M.R.I.A. Those Charters which have not already appeared in print will be edited by the Rev. JAMES GRAVES, A.B., M.R.I.A. Imperial 4to, cloth extra, gilt, 36s. [*Nearly Ready.*

WESTWOOD'S PALÆOGRAPHIA SACRA PICTORIA:
being a Series of Illustrations of the Ancient Versions of the Bible, copied from
Illuminated Manuscripts, executed between the Fourth and Sixteenth Centuries.
Royal 4to, with 50 beautifully Illuminated Plates, half-bound morocco, £3 10s.

WILSON'S AMERICAN ORNITHOLOGY ; or, Natural History
of the Birds of the United States; with a Continuation by Prince CHARLES
LUCIEN BONAPARTE. NEW AND ENLARGED EDITION, completed by the
insertion of above One Hundred Birds omitted in the original Work, and Illustrated by valuable Notes, and Life of the Author, by Sir WILLIAM JARDINE.
Three Vols., 8vo, with a fine Portrait of WILSON, and 97 Plates, exhibiting 363
figures of Birds, accurately engraved, and most beautifully coloured, on glazed
drawing-paper, half-bound morocco, gilt.   [*In the press.*
"The History of American Birds by Alexander Wilson is equal in elegance to the
most distinguished of our own splendid works on Ornithology."—CUVIER.
" This is by far the best edition of the American Ornithology, both on account of
the beautiful plates and the interesting notes of the editor. Every ornithologist
must of course possess the work, and he should if possible procure this edition."—
NEVILLE WOOD.

WILSON'S FRENCH-ENGLISH AND ENGLISH-FRENCH
DICTIONARY ; containing full Explanations, Definitions, Synonyms, Idioms,
Proverbs, Terms of Art and Science, and Rules for the Pronunciation of each
Language. Compiled from the Dictionaries of the French Academy, BOYER,
CHAMBAUD, GARNIER, LAVEAUX, DES CARRIÈRES and FAIN, JOHNSON, and
WALKER. Imperial 8vo, 1,323 closely-printed pages, cloth extra, 15s.

WONDERFUL CHARACTERS : Memoirs and Anecdotes of
Remarkable and Eccentric Persons of every Age and Nation. By HENRY
WILSON and JAMES CAULFIELD. Crown 8vo, cloth extra, with 61 full-page
Engravings, 7s. 6d.

WRIGHT'S (Andrew) COURT-HAND RESTORED; or, Stu-
dent's Assistant in Reading Old Deeds, Charters, Records, &c. Folio, half-
morocco, 10s. 6d.

WRIGHT'S CARICATURE HISTORY of the GEORGES
(House of Hanover). With 400 Pictures, Caricatures, Squibs, Broadsides,
Window Pictures, &c. By THOMAS WRIGHT, Esq., M.A., F.S.A. Crown 8vo,
cloth extra, 7s. 6d.
" Emphatically one of the liveliest of books, as also one of the most interesting.
Has the twofold merit of being at once amusing and edifying."—*Morning Post.*

YANKEE DROLLERIES. Edited, with Introduction, by GEORGE
AUGUSTUS SALA. In Three Parts—the FIRST containing ARTEMUS WARD'S
BOOK, the BIGLOW PAPERS, ORPHEUS C. KERR, JACK DOWNING, and the
NASBY PAPERS ; the SECOND containing ARTEMUS WARD'S TRAVELS, HANS
BREITMANN, PROFESSOR AT THE BREAKFAST TABLE, the BIGLOW PAPERS
(Part II.), and JOSH BILLINGS ; the THIRD containing ARTEMUS WARD AMONG
THE FENIANS, AUTOCRAT OF THE BREAKFAST TABLE, BRET HARTE'S STORIES,
THE INNOCENTS ABROAD, and THE NEW PILGRIM'S PROGRESS. Three Vols.,
crown 8vo, cloth extra, gilt, price 10s. 6d.; or, separately, 3s. 6d. per vol.

C-295-C

6

J. OGDEN AND CO., PRINTERS, 172, ST. JOHN STREET, LONDON.